सीताराम

Ramashtakam

&

Rama Jayam - Likhita Japam Mala

:

Journal for Writing the Rama-Nama
100,000 Times alongside the Sacred Hindu Text
Ramashtakam,
with English Translation & Transliteration

::

श्रीरामाष्टकम्

व

राम जयम - लिखित जपम

राम-नाम लेखन माला

(एक लाख राम-नाम लेखन हेतु)

Belongs to ____

Published by: **Rama-Nama Journals**
(an Imprint of e1i1 Corporation)

Title: **Ramashtakam & Rama Jayam - Likhita Japam Mala**
Sub-Title: **Journal for Writing the Rama-Nama 100,000 Times alongside the Sacred Hindu Text Ramashtakam, with English Translation & Transliteration**

Author: **Sushma**

Parts of this book have been derived/inspired from our other publication:
"Rama Hymns" (Authored by Sushma)

Identifiers

ISBN: **978-1-945739-17-0** (Paperback)

—o—

www.**e1i1**.com -- www.**OnlyRama**.com
email: **e1i1***books***e1i1**@gmail.com

Our books can be bought online, or at Amazon, or any bookstore. If a book is not available at your neighborhood bookstore they will be happy to order it for you. (Certain Hardcover Editions may not be immediately available—we apologize)

Some of our Current/Forthcoming Books are listed below. Please note that this is a partial list and that we are continually adding new books.
Please visit www.**e1i1**.com / www.**onlyRama**.com for current offerings.

- **Tulsi Ramayana—The Hindu Bible:** Ramcharitmanas with English Translation & Transliteration
- **Tulsi-Ramayana Rama-Nama Mala (multiple volumes):** Legacy Journals for Writing the Rama Name alongside Tulsidas Ramcharitmanas—contains English Translation & Transliteration, Inspirational Quotes of Hindu saints, and space for you to jot down your spiritual sentiments on a daily basis. Once embellished with your Rama-Namas, these books become priceless treasures which you can present to your loved ones—a true gift of love, labor, caring, wishing, and above all—Devotion.
- **Ramcharitmanas:** Ramayana of Tulsidas with Transliteration (in English)
- **Ramayana, Large**: Tulsi Ramcharitmanas, Hindi only Edition, Large Font and Paper size
- **Ramayana, Medium**: Tulsi Ramcharitmanas, Hindi only Edition, Medium Font and Paper size
- **Ramayana, Small**: Tulsi Ramcharitmanas, Hindi only Edition, Small Font and Paper size
- **Sundarakanda:** The Fifth-Ascent of Tulsi Ramayana
- **RAMA GOD:** In the Beginning - Upanishad Vidya (Know Thyself)
- **Purling Shadows:** And A Dream Called Life - Upanishad Vidya (Know Thyself)
- **Fiery Circle:** Upanishad Vidya (Know Thyself)
- **Rama Hymns:** Hanuman-Chalisa, Rama-Raksha-Stotra, Bhushumdi-Ramayana, Nama-Ramayanam, Rama-Shata-Nama-Stotra, etc. with Transliteration & English Translation
- **Rama Jayam - Likhita Japam Mala alongside Sacred Hindu Texts (several):** Journals for Writing the Rama Name 100,000 Times alongside various Hindu Texts, with English Translation & Transliteration. Embellish these Books with your Rama-Namas and they become transformed into priceless treasures which you can later gift to your loved ones.
- **Rama Jayam - Likhita Japam Mala alongside Rama-Mantras (several):** Journals for Writing the Rama Name 100,000 Times alongside the Rama-Mantras from one lettered to thirty-two others. Embellish these with your Rama-Namas and they become transformed into priceless treasures.

-- On our website may be found links to renditions of Rama Hymns –
-- Rama Mantras/Hymns/Pictures are also available printed on Quality Shirts from Amazon. See our website for details --

rāma-nāma mahimā

In this modern era—which is awash with the six *Gunas* of Māyā: *Kāma* (Lust), *Krodha* (Anger), *Lobha* (Greed), *Moha* (Infatuation), *Mada* (Pride) & *Mātsarya* (Envy)—we find our minds sinking in worldliness. It seems that despite their best intent, no one can remain unsullied from the taints of Kali; this appears to be the fait-accompli of the *Kali-Yuga*—a very sad fate indeed. But despair not, because there is hope—we find ourselves assured.

The Japa of Rāma-Nāma (Rāma-Name) is the supreme path to salvation in this *Kali-Yuga*, assure our Scriptures; there is no Dharma higher than Nāma-Dharma in this Age of Kali—we are told. Sing the praises of the Lord and remain engaged in *Nāma-Smarana*—is the advice given to us by our saints. The chanting of Rāma-Nāma is The-One-Supreme-Path to escape the clutches of *Kali-Yuga*—declares Rāmacharit*m*ānas—and in fact it **is the one and only Dharma which is easy and feasible in the present times.**

Many of the Hindu saints zealously assert: "In this Kali-Yuga, there is no other means, no other means, no other means of salvation—other than chanting the holy name Rāma, chanting the holy name Rāma, chanting the holy name Rāma."

Rāma-Japa—the constant repetition of the **Supreme-Mantra 'Rāma'**—is usually done mentally, or on a rosary; but there is one extremely efficacious method of this Japa: the *Likhita-Japa*, or the Written-Chant.

The practice of writing the Rāma Mantra over and over on paper is called the *Likhita-Japa*. This written form of Japa is a lasting record of your chant, remaining ever imbued with those holy vibrations, for all times, for the benefit of you and the future generations.

In India, as you may know, devotees of God have been chanting the name 'Rāma' and writing the Name 'Rāma'—pages upon pages of it, running into billions and billions, for ages. Hindu children are taught to write the Rāma-Nāma from their very childhood, and the writing competitions of the One *Lakh* Rāma–Nāma, brings up nostalgic memories for many Hindus.

The completed Rāma-Nāma books are variously utilized. Some devotees preserve them carefully for their holy association and divine energy, while others donate them to temples. The written Rāma-Nāma Books are used in the foundations of temples during construction; they add divine energy to the Temples—while in turn strengthening the foundations of the spiritual life of those who wrote the Rāma Name. Also some collected Rāma-Nāma books are placed in crypts to be used during *Yagna's* in Rāma Temples; and temples preserve these books for future. Devotees also place their own written Rāma-Nāma Books during the laying of foundation of their new homes, or in their *Pooja*-Room.

Of those of our Chakras (psychic centers), where our *Sanchit* (accumulated) Karmas are stored, Rāma is the *Beej Mantra*. The writing of Rāma-Nāma helps cleanse the Chakras, and our suppressed emotions, and the negative *Sanskaras* of the subconscious, and our remnant/unworked Karmas from past lives—which all get purged through the repetition of the Rāma-Nāma Mantra.

The chanting of Rāma-Nāma is a direct way to liberation. As per belief, devotees attempt to write down at least Eighty-Four Lakh (84,00,000) Rāma-Nāmas to get out of the birth-death cycle of Eighty-Four Lakh *Yonīs*, and thereby attain to salvation.

The *Likhita* Rāma-Nāma Japa is a powerful and transformative tool. As you write the Rāma-Nāma, all the senses become engaged in the service of Lord-God, and you find yourself simultaneously chanting and hearing and contemplating on the Lord—everything comes together naturally. This method clears away your thoughts and helps concentrate the entirety of your soul upon the Divine.

Any Japa is beneficial but somehow writing the Rāma-Nāma on paper brings up a great singularity of focus within the mind—and the peace of heart which ensues is something which is not so easily achieved with other forms of Japa. The written form of Rāma-Japa is somehow able to engage those parts of our body-mind continuum which other methods can not—and our meditative stance is able to achieve much deeper levels.

There is something special which will happen when you write the Rāma-Nāma—as you will discover. Peace and tranquility will surround you as you write the Supreme-Mantra: Rāma. The Rāma-Nāma will impart to you supreme strength, and great tolerance to withstand the vicissitudes of life. Bright unclouded wisdom will illumine your mind. You will find yourself in complete sense of surrender to your inner being. The resonance of God will resonate throughout your mind-body continuity. You will feel a flux of divine energy resonating within you. You will get great power and peace in your everyday life. The chanting of Rāma Mantra will protect your inner world as well as the outside.

Although the Rāma-Mantra is the gateway to higher consciousness and spiritual upliftment, but even at such junctures—when you find yourself in odd situations, where all the paths seem blocked—then just walking away from everything and simply writing the Rāma Nāma, will give you much needed clarity of thought—and a divine inspiration that will show the way out.

Thus, the Rāma Nāma is very transformative: with it you gain a balanced progress in your outside world and the inner. *Sant* Tulsidās says in *Rāmacharitmānas*: Place the Rāma-Nāma Jewel at the threshold, and there will be light both inside and out; i.e. a constant chant of the Rāma-Nāma from the mouth—the doorway to the body—will bring you external materialistic wellbeing, and also an inner spiritual wellness—both. Incredibly, with the Rāma-Nāma, you get to have the best of both the worlds.

According to the Vedas, just as the sun dispels the darkness, the chanting of Rāma-Nāma dispels all the evils and obstacles of life. The Rāma Nāma cures agony and showers the blessings of God; all righteous wishes get fulfilled; jealousy and pride disappear; life becomes imbued with satisfaction and peace; all of life's needs fall in place automatically—just like a miracle of nature guiding nature's forces. You may not always get what you want in the exact same form, but the Rāma-Nāma will purify things and bring to you the same needed happiness and bliss in a much more refined and lasting way. Your life will truly become filled with tranquility. Thus, with the Rāma-Nāma, an immense sense of spiritual wellbeing is experienced apart from gain of material happiness.

For *Likhita* Japa, you can write the Rāma-Nāma in any language of your choice—after all, Name is the connecting chord between the Divine and your inner self—but writing the Rāma-Nāma in its original Sanskrit form is simply superlative—most excellent, most effective. Sanskrit is *Deva-Bhāshā* (the language-of-gods). If you do not know how to write **राम** in Sanskrit it is quite easy. In the figure below, trace the contours 1-2 (which is the sound of underlined letters in the word ‘**ru**n’), 3-4 (the sound of underlined letter a in ‘**a**rk’), 5-6 & 7-8 (the underlined mu in ‘**mu**st’) and lastly the line 9-10; and that’s it. Note the similarity of English **R** , **M** to the Sanskrit **र** , **म** , (and English words used here like *Name, Saint*—similar to the Sanskrit *Nāma, Sant.*) All European languages have their roots in Sanskrit, the great grand mother tongue of most.

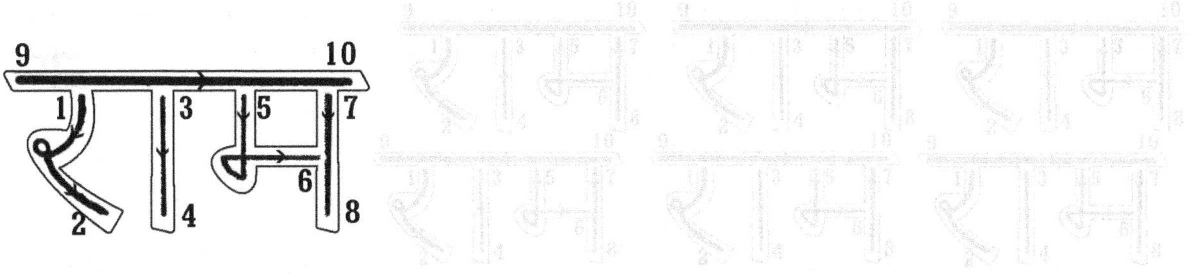

Write the Supreme-Mantra Rāma with reverence, every day, preferably at a set time, or as and when possible, in small measures, or copiously—howsoever your situation permits. There are no hard rules, do what feels good to your Soul. The important thing is to engage in the *Likhita*-Japa. When completed, you could keep the books in your Worship-Room, preserve them as treasures to pass on to future generations, donate them to Rāma Temples, or gift them to your loved ones—who will thereby inculcate crucial values from you, and learn the importance of the Rāma-Nāma, and get inspired with Hindu Values, especially so the younger ones.

While writing, focus your mind on the Rāma-Name and chant it within. Imagine Sītā-Rāma showering you with their bliss. Try to stay free of distractions, and with time you will find that your mind will take a natural meditative stance while engaged in the written Rāma-Nāma Japa.

You can choose any notebook or paper to write on, not necessarily this one. Traditionally people will write the Rāma Name in red ink on straight lines; but some devotees will also simultaneously make an interesting design—by changing the orientation of lines, or using different colors, utilizing an underlying outline to base their Japa upon. Do what comes naturally; no hard rules.

Find a set of pencils or pens which write and feel beautiful to you. If making an intricate pattern use pens that have finer points—but see that the ink does not bleed through to the other side.

Ideally, you will have a special set of pens kept purely for the Likhita Japa. This will make it easier for you to enter into the spirit of things. You will find that such implements—which you habitually use for holy tasks—build up energy and holy resonance.

A grid of 21 by 48 (1008 boxes) is provided for you as a guide—to be able to write a thousand Rāma Names per page. Some people will ignore the boxes and write in their own style, as and how their own inspiration leads them, creating their own design on the pages; and sometimes the design will preclude using all the boxes; but still, with 108 pages to write upon, and with space for 1008 names per page, you should be able to cross the 100,000 Rāma-Nāma objective of the book. The 100,000 target is merely suggestive—it assumes you write one Rāma-Nāma per box; obviously your mileage will vary, and you will get a figure more or less than 100,000, depending upon if you write smaller or larger. If need be, please utilize the empty spaces on the pages.

The pages contain the śrī-rāmāṣṭakam (8 verses on Rāma) Text as font outlines. Before beginning your Likhita Japa for that page, if you can write within the rāmāṣṭakam outlines the Rāma-Nāmas—using color/size/slant which is different from the outside—then it will make those Verses stand out. Or if you cannot write so tiny, then simply color the verses using colored pencil or highlighter—that way the Text will pop out from amongst the waves of surrounding Rāma-Nāmas. We wish you Happy Rāma-Nāma Japa.

Once embellished with your Rāma-Nāmas, this śrī-rāmāṣṭakam book will become a priceless treasure which you can present to your loved ones—an unparalleled gift of love, labor, caring, wishing, and above all—Devotion.

—o—o—o—o—o—o—o—o—o—o—o—

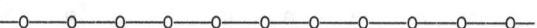

राम राम

राम
राम
राम
राम
राम
राम
राम
राम
राम
राम
राम
राम
राम
राम
राम
राम
राम
राम
राम
राम
राम
राम
राम
राम
राम
राम
राम
राम
राम
राम
राम
राम
राम
राम
राम
राम
राम
राम
राम
राम
राम
राम
राम
राम
राम
राम
राम
राम

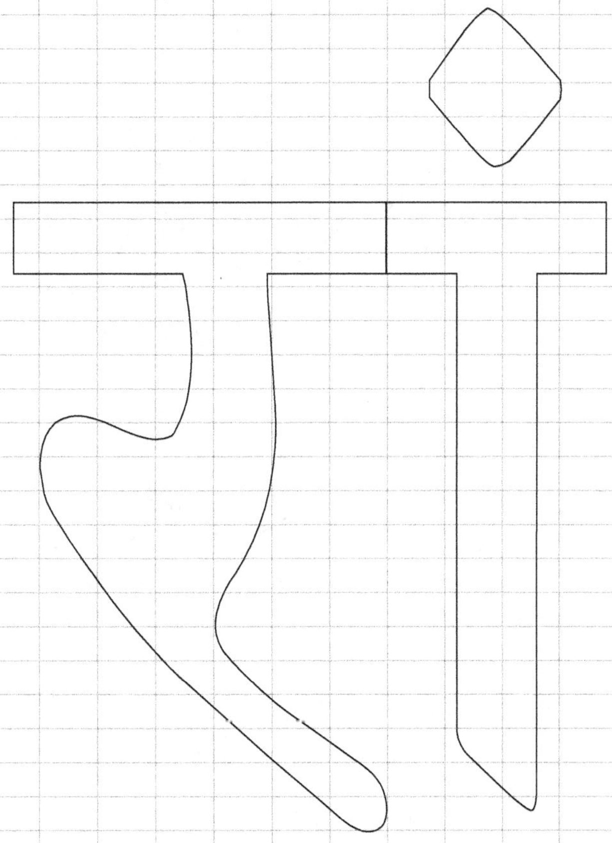

Today's Date : ____________________

राम राम

राम
राम
राम
राम
राम
राम
राम
राम
राम
राम
राम
राम
राम
राम
राम
राम
राम
राम
राम
राम
राम
राम
राम
राम
राम
राम
राम
राम
राम
राम
राम
राम
राम
राम
राम
राम
राम
राम
राम
राम
राम
राम
राम
राम
राम
राम
राम
राम

Today's Date

राम राम

राम
राम
राम
राम
राम
राम
राम
राम
राम
राम
राम
राम
राम
राम
राम
राम
राम
राम
राम
राम
राम
राम
राम
राम
राम
राम
राम
राम
राम
राम
राम
राम
राम
राम
राम
राम
राम
राम
राम
राम
राम
राम
राम
राम
राम
राम
राम
राम

राम

राम राम

रां राम

राम
राम
राम
राम
राम
राम
राम
राम
राम
राम
राम
राम
राम
राम
राम
राम
राम
राम
राम
राम
राम
राम
राम
राम
राम
राम
राम
राम
राम
राम
राम
राम
राम
राम
राम
राम
राम
राम
राम
राम
राम
राम
राम
राम
राम
राम
राम
राम

Today's Date

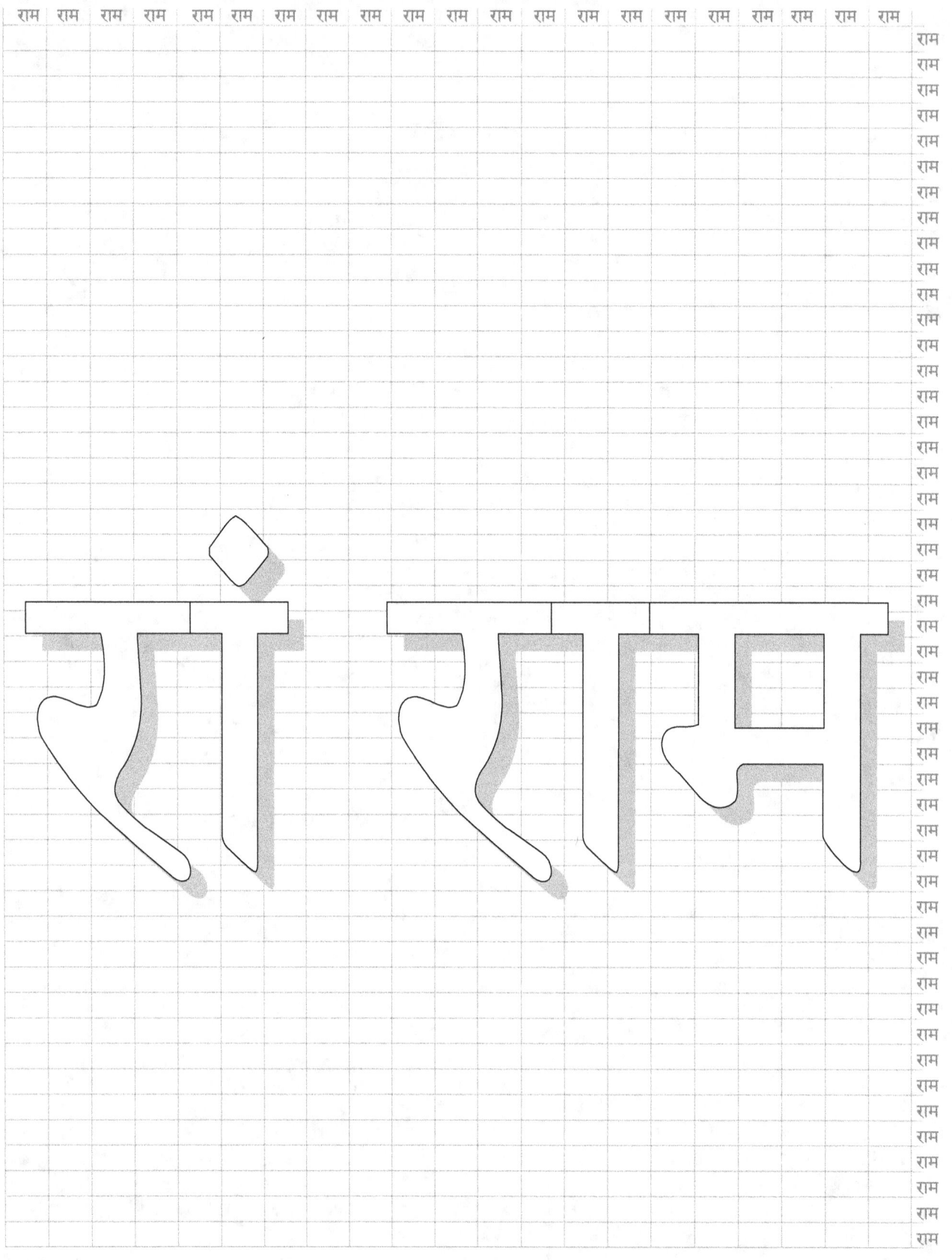

राम राम

राम
राम
राम
राम
राम
राम
राम
राम
राम
राम
राम
राम
राम
राम
राम
राम
राम
राम
राम
राम
राम
राम

ॐ राम

राम
राम
राम
राम
राम
राम
राम
राम
राम
राम
राम
राम
राम
राम
राम
राम
राम
राम
राम
राम
राम
राम
राम
राम
राम
राम

Today's Date : ____________________

राम राम

रामचंद्र

राम
राम
राम
राम
राम
राम
राम
राम
राम
राम
राम
राम
राम
राम
राम
राम
राम
राम
राम
राम
राम
राम
राम
राम
राम
राम
राम
राम
राम
राम
राम
राम
राम
राम
राम
राम
राम
राम
राम
राम
राम
राम
राम
राम
राम
राम
राम
राम

_______________ Today's Date

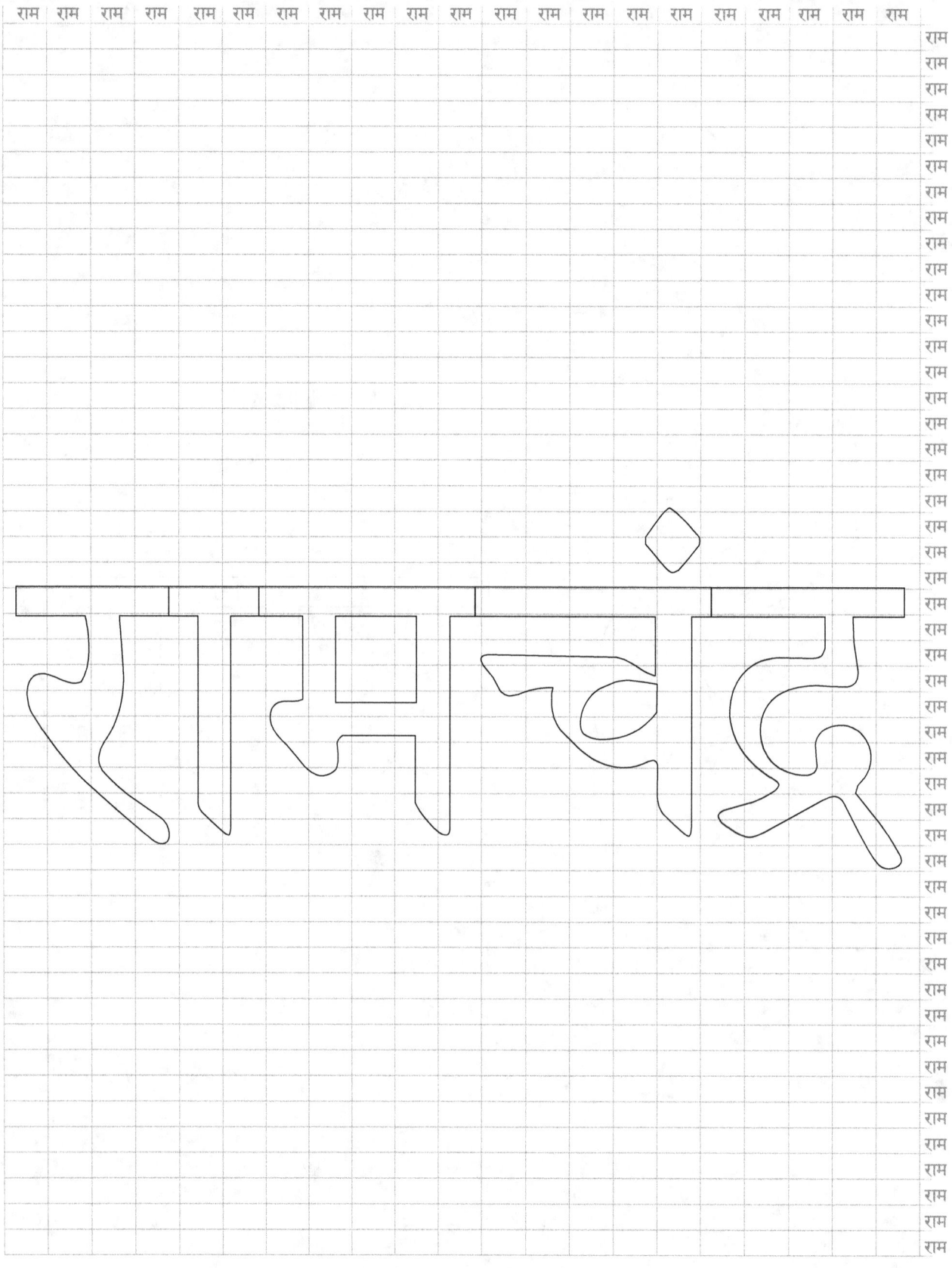

राम राम

राम
राम
राम
राम
राम
राम
राम
राम
राम
राम
राम
राम
राम
राम
राम
राम
राम
राम
राम
राम
राम
राम
राम

रामभद्र

राम
राम
राम
राम
राम
राम
राम
राम
राम
राम
राम
राम
राम
राम
राम
राम
राम
राम
राम
राम
राम
राम
राम
राम
राम
राम
राम
राम
राम
राम

Today's Date : ____________________

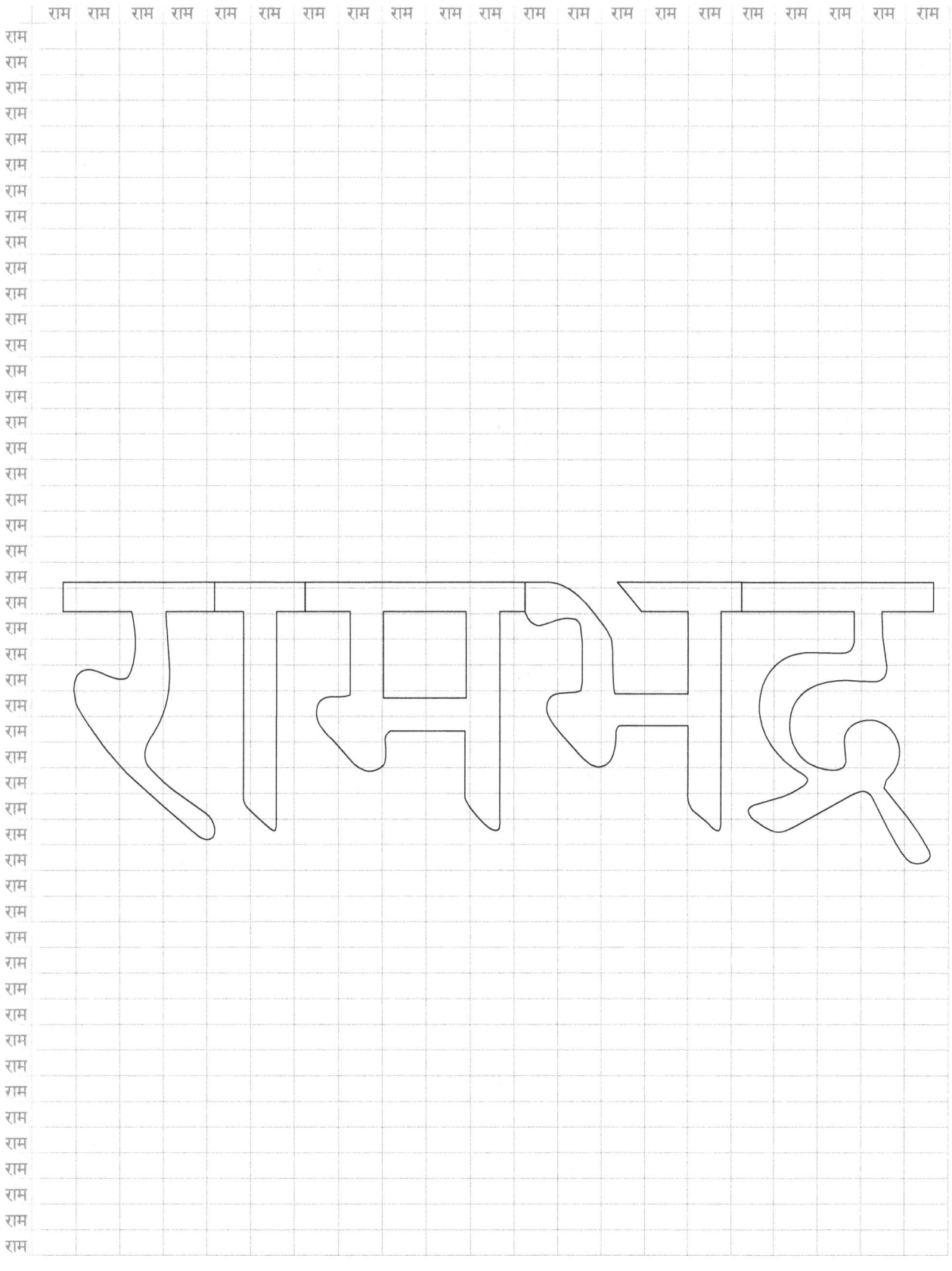

राम राम

राम
राम
राम
राम
राम
राम
राम
राम
राम
राम
राम
राम
राम
राम
राम
राम
राम
राम
राम
राम
राम
राम
राम
राम
राम
राम
राम
राम
राम
राम
राम
राम
राम
राम
राम
राम
राम
राम
राम
राम
राम
राम
राम
राम
राम
राम
राम
राम

अथ

श्री

रामाष्टकम्

__________ Today's Date

राम राम

राम राम

atha śrī rāmāṣṭakam

(Now commences rāmāṣṭakam)

राम राम

राम
राम
राम
राम
राम
राम
राम
राम
राम
राम
राम
राम
राम
राम
राम
राम
राम
राम
राम
राम
राम
राम
राम
राम
राम
राम
राम
राम
राम
राम
राम
राम
राम
राम
राम
राम
राम
राम
राम
राम
राम
राम
राम
राम
राम
राम
राम
राम

भजे विशेषसुन्दरं

bhaje viśeṣa sundaraṁ

______________ Today's Date

राम राम

राम
राम
राम
राम
राम
राम
राम
राम
राम
राम
राम
राम
राम
राम
राम
राम

समस्तपापखण्डनम्

राम
राम
राम
राम
राम
राम
राम
राम
राम
राम
राम
राम
राम
राम

samasta pāpa khaṇḍanam

राम
राम
राम
राम
राम
राम
राम
राम
राम
राम
राम
राम
राम
राम
राम

Today's Date : ____________________

राम राम

राम राम

स्वभक्तचित्तरञ्जनं

svabhakta cittarañjanaṁ

भजे विशेषसुन्दरं समस्तपापखण्डनम् ।

bhaje viśeṣa sundaraṁ samasta pāpa khaṇḍa nam ,

स्वभक्तचित्तरञ्जनं सदैव राममद्वयम् ॥ १ ॥

sva bhakta citta rañja naṁ sa daiva rāmam ad vayam .1.

_______________ Today's Date

राम राम

राम राम

सदैव राममद्वयम्

sadaiva rāmam advayam

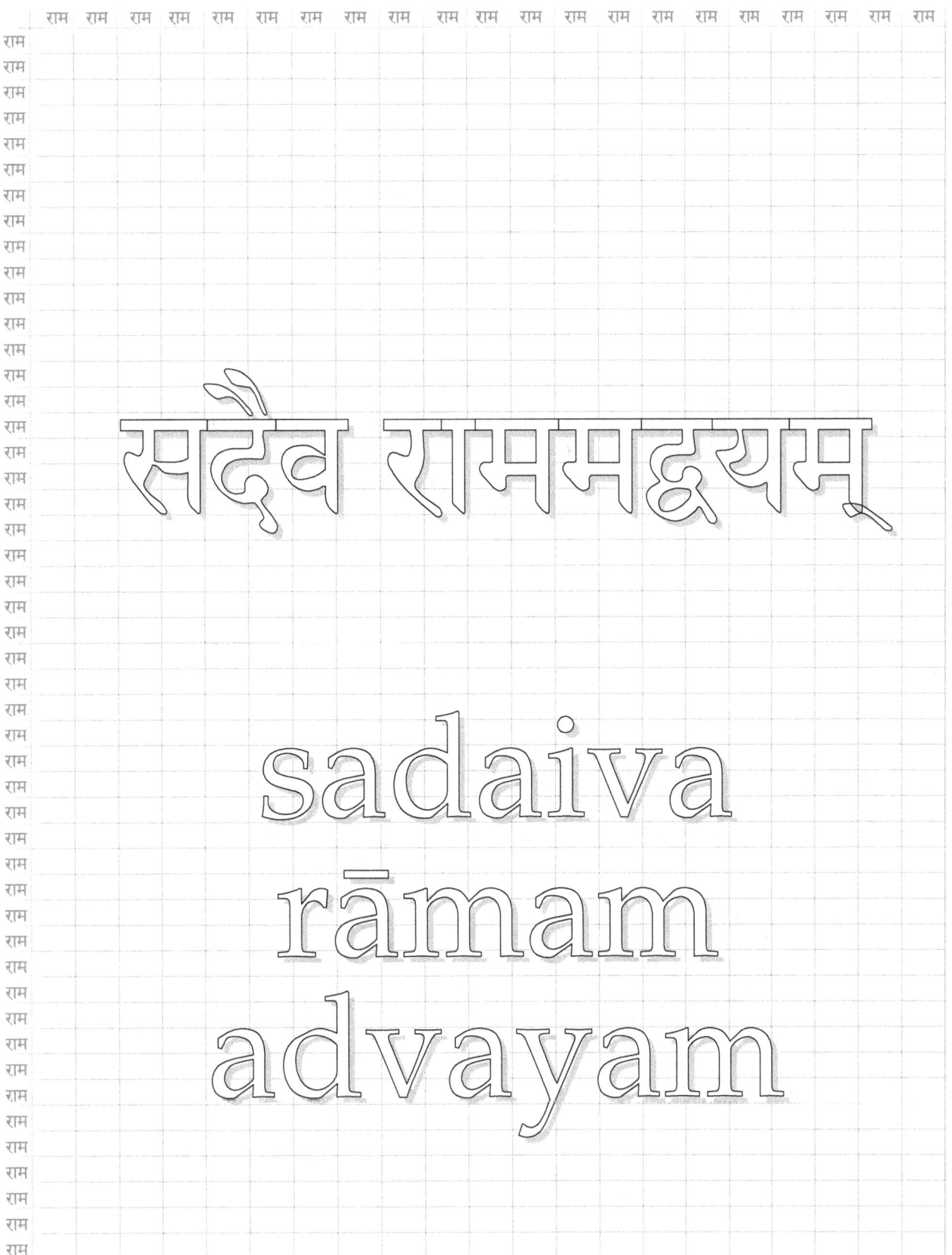

He, who annihilates all sins, who brings lasting joy to the hearts of His devotees, O mind, dwell upon Him—the supremely beautiful Lord: Shrī Rāma, the One-God second to none.

राम राम

जटाकलापशोभितं

jaṭākalāpa śobhitaṁ

______________ Today's Date

राम राम

राम
राम
राम
राम
राम
राम
राम
राम
राम
राम
राम
राम
राम
राम
राम
राम
राम
राम
राम
राम
राम
राम
राम
राम
राम
राम
राम
राम
राम
राम
राम
राम
राम
राम
राम
राम
राम
राम
राम
राम
राम
राम
राम
राम
राम
राम
राम
राम

समस्तपापनाशकम्

samasta
pāpa
nāśakam

राम राम
राम राम

स्वभक्तभीतिभङ्गनं

svabhakta bhīti bhaṅjanaṁ

जटाकलापशोभितं समस्तपापनाशकम् ।
jaṭā kalā paśo bhitaṁ samasta pāpa nāśa kam ,
स्वभक्तभीतिभङ्गनं भजे ह राममद्वयम् ॥ २ ॥
sva bhakta bhīti bhaṅja naṁ bhaje ha rāmam ad vayam .2.

_______________ Today's Date

राम राम

भजे ह राममद्वयम्

bhaje ha rāmam advayam

He, who is the destroyers of sins, who dispels all fears from the hearts of His devotees, O mind, dwell upon His resplendent form with matted hair—Him Shrī Rāma, the One-God second to none.

राम राम

निजस्वरूपबोधकं

nija svarūpa bodhakaṁ

राम राम

Today's Date

राम राम

राम राम

कृपाकरं भवापहम्

kṛpākaraṁ bhavāpaham

राम राम

राम राम

समं शिवं निरञ्जनं

samaṁ śivaṁ nirañjanaṁ

निजस्वरूपबोधकं कृपाकरं भवापहम् ।

nija svarūpa bodha kaṁ kṛpā karaṁ bhav āpaham ,

समं शिवं निरञ्जनं भजे ह राममद्वयम् ॥ ३ ॥

samaṁ śivaṁ nirañja naṁ bhaje ha rāmam ad vayam .3.

Today's Date

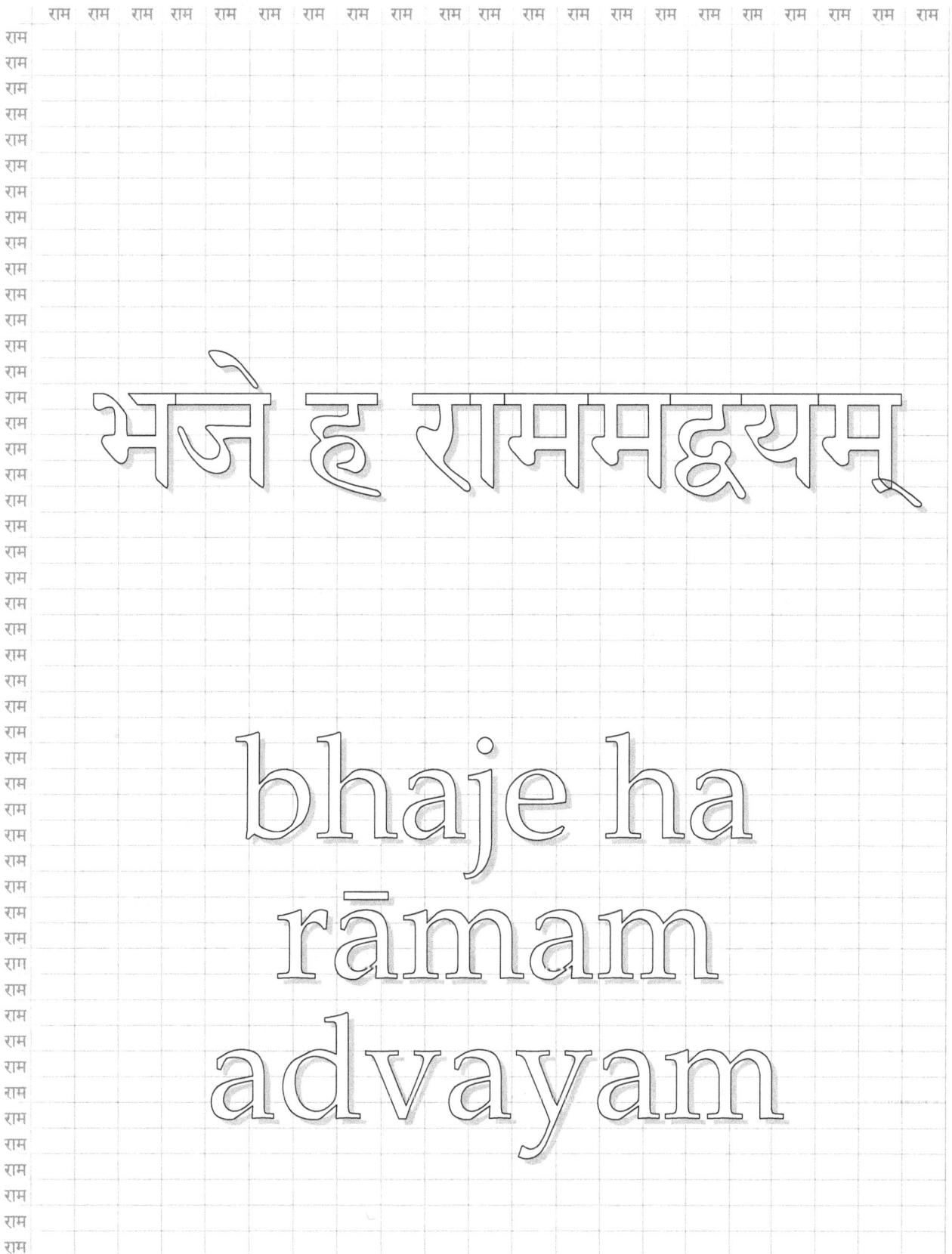

भजे ह राममद्वयम्

bhaje ha rāmam advayam

Through whom we become enlightened of our true nature, who is most merciful & kind, who takes us across this intimidating ocean-like world, who is equitable to all, who is ever auspicious, ever pure—O mind, dwell upon the ocean of tranquility Shrī Rāma, the One-God second to none.

राम राम

राम
राम
राम
राम
राम
राम
राम
राम
राम
राम
राम
राम
राम
राम
राम
राम
राम
राम
राम
राम
राम
राम
राम
राम
राम
राम
राम
राम
राम
राम
राम
राम
राम
राम
राम
राम
राम
राम
राम
राम
राम
राम
राम
राम
राम
राम
राम
राम

सहप्रपञ्चकल्पितं

sahaprapañca kalpitaṁ

______________ Today's Date

राम राम

ह्यनामरूपवास्तवम्

hyanāmarūpa
vāstavam

राम राम

राम राम

निराकृतिं निरामयं

nirākṛtiṁ nirāmayaṁ

सहप्रपञ्चकल्पितं ह्यनामरूपवास्तवम् ।

saha pra pañca kalpitaṁ hya nāma rūpa vāsta vam ,

निराकृतिं निरामयं भजे ह राममद्वयम् ॥ ४ ॥

nir ākṛtiṁ nir āmayaṁ bhaje ha rāmam ad vayam .4.

Today's Date

राम राम

भजे ह राममद्वयम्

bhaje ha rāmam advayam

Of His will who took this illusory form—who is the world, from whom is the world, who has the world within Him—who is the Absolute-Truth, without a name, without a form, free from blemishes, shortcomings, faults—I worship Him: Shri Rāma, the One-God second to none.

Today's Date : ____________

राम राम

राम
राम
राम
राम
राम
राम
राम
राम
राम
राम
राम
राम
राम
राम
राम
राम
राम
राम
राम
राम
राम
राम
राम
राम
राम
राम
राम
राम
राम
राम
राम
राम
राम
राम
राम
राम
राम
राम
राम
राम
राम
राम
राम
राम
राम
राम
राम
राम

निष्प्रपञ्चनिर्विकल्प

niṣprapañca nirvikalpa

______________ Today's Date

राम राम

निर्मलं निरामयम्

nirmalaṁ nirāmayam

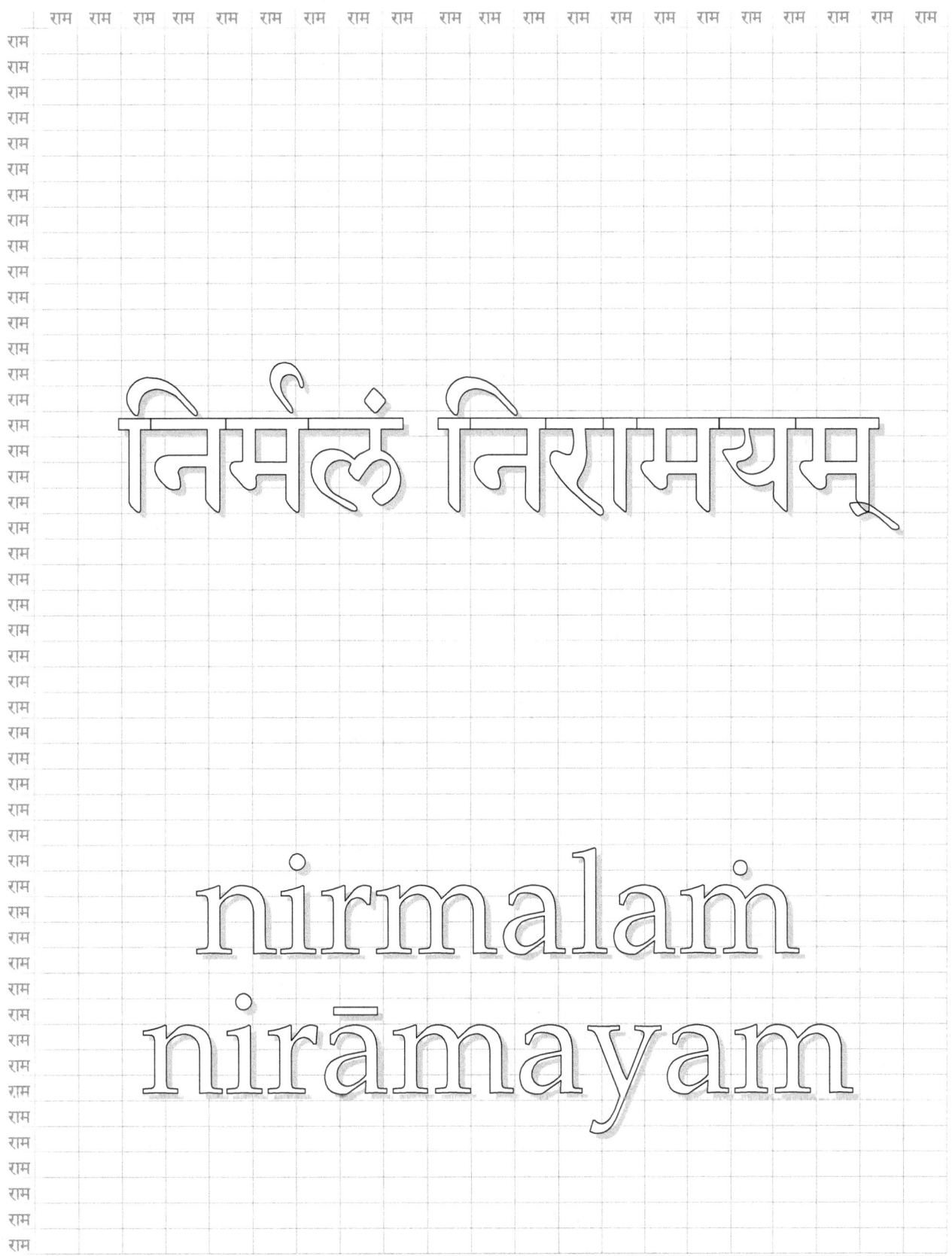

राम राम
राम राम

चिदेकरूपसन्ततं

cidekarūpa santataṁ

निष्प्रपञ्चनिर्विकल्पनिर्मलं निरामयम् ॥
niṣ prapañca nir vikalpa nir malaṁ nirāma yam.
चिदेकरूपसन्ततं भजे ह राममद्वयम् ॥ ५ ॥
cid eka rūpa santa taṁ bhaje ha rāmam ad vayam .5.

_______________ Today's Date

राम राम

राम
राम
राम
राम
राम
राम
राम
राम
राम
राम
राम
राम
राम
राम
राम
राम
राम
राम
राम
राम
राम
राम
राम
राम
राम
राम
राम
राम
राम
राम
राम
राम
राम
राम
राम
राम
राम
राम
राम
राम
राम
राम
राम
राम
राम
राम
राम
राम

भजे ह राममद्वयम्

bhaje ha rāmam advayam

O mind, dwell on Rāma—the imperishable essence beyond creation, beyond the worldly dualities, untainted, the ever pure, unsullied of worldly maladies, the absolute Truth that stands as the all-abiding essence within everything—O mind, worship Rāma, the One-God second to none.

राम राम

राम
राम
राम
राम
राम
राम
राम
राम
राम
राम
राम
राम
राम
राम
राम
राम
राम
राम
राम
राम
राम
राम
राम
राम
राम
राम
राम
राम
राम
राम
राम
राम
राम
राम
राम
राम
राम
राम
राम
राम
राम
राम
राम
राम
राम
राम
राम
राम
राम
राम

भवाब्धिपोतरूपकं

bhavābdhi pota rūpakaṁ

_______________ Today's Date

ह्यशेषदेहकल्पितम्

hyaśeṣadeha
kalpitam

राम राम

राम राम

गुणाकरं कृपाकरं

guṇākaraṁ kṛpākaraṁ

भवाब्धिपोतरूपकं ह्यशेषदेहकल्पितम् ।

bhav ābdhi pota rūpa kaṁ hya śeṣa deha kal pitam ,

गुणाकरं कृपाकरं भजे ह राममद्वयम् ॥ ६ ॥

guṇā karaṁ kṛpā karaṁ bhaje ha rāmam ad vayam .6.

_______________ Today's Date

राम राम

राम राम

भजे ह राममद्वयम्

bhaje ha rāmam advayam

Who is the bark to cross the ocean of worldly existence, the One-shining Truth behind all beingness, doer behind all activity—Him venerate: the all-merciful all-gracious fount of virtues Shrī Rāma, the One-God second to none.

Today's Date : ____________________

राम राम

राम राम

महावाक्यबोधकै

mahāvākya bodhakair

Today's Date

राम राम

विराजमानवाक्पदैः

virājamana vākpadaiḥ

राम राम

राम राम

परब्रह्म व्यापकं

parabrahma vyāpakaṁ

महावाक्यबोधकैर्विराजमनवाक्पदैः ।
mahā vākya bodha kair virāja mana vāk padaiḥ ,
परब्रह्म व्यापकं भजे ह राममद्वयम् ॥ ७ ॥
para brahma vyāpa kaṁ bhaje ha rāmam ad vayam .7.

_______________ Today's Date

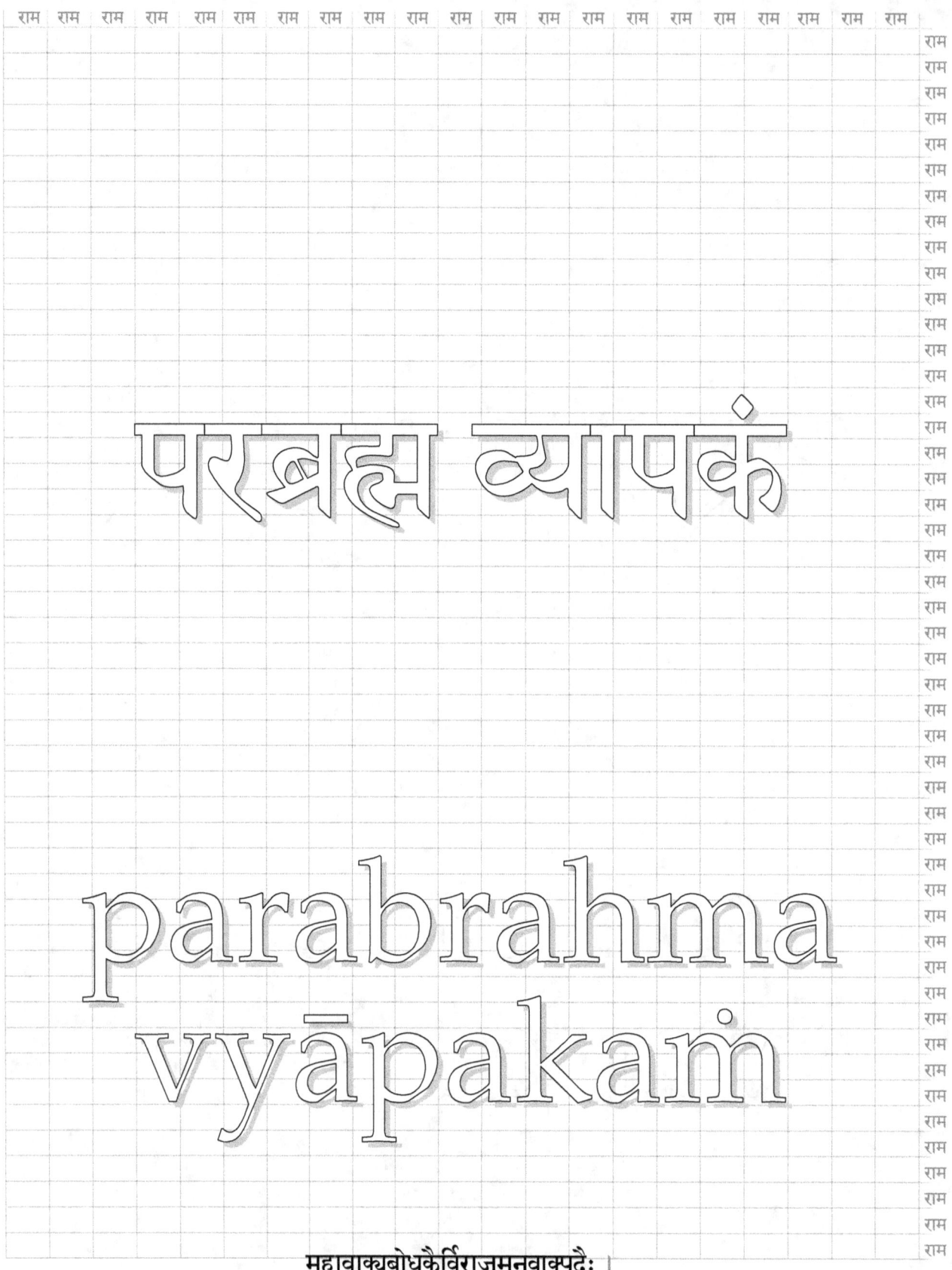

भजे ह राममद्वयम्

bhaje ha
rāmam
advayam

Worship Shrī Rāma—the essence of Vedanta, whose glory irradiates through the great Vedic Sayings, who is the Supreme all-pervading Brahmm diffused throughout the universe—the Exalted One Rāma, the One-God second to none.

राम राम

राम राम

शिवप्रदं सुखप्रदं

śivapradaṁ sukhapradaṁ

__________________ Today's Date

भवच्छिदं भ्रमापहम्

bhavacchidaṁ
bhramāpaham

राम राम

राम राम

विराजमानदैशिकं

virājamāna daiśikaṁ

शिवप्रदं सुखप्रदं भवच्छिदं भ्रमापहम् ।
śiva pradaṁ sukha pradaṁ bhav acchid aṁ bhram āpaham ,
विराजमानदैशिकं भजे ह राममद्वयम् ॥ ८ ॥
virāja māna daiśik aṁ bhaje ha rāmam ad vayam .8.

_______________ Today's Date

राम राम

राम राम

भजे ह राममद्वयम्

bhaje ha rāmam advayam

Who confers felicity and prosperity, who rents asunder all worldly bondages, who is beyond the delusive Māyā, who is the Supreme-Self dwelling within His own resplendency—Him worship, Shrī Rāma, the One-God second to none.

Today's Date : ____________________

राम राम

रामाष्टकं पठति यः

rāmāṣṭakaṁ
paṭhati yaḥ

राम
राम
राम
राम
राम
राम
राम
राम
राम
राम
राम
राम
राम
राम
राम
राम
राम
राम
राम
राम
राम
राम
राम
राम
राम
राम
राम
राम
राम
राम
राम
राम
राम
राम
राम
राम
राम
राम
राम
राम
राम
राम
राम
राम
राम
राम
राम
राम

_______________ Today's Date

सुकरं सुपुण्यं

sukaraṁ
supuṇyaṁ

राम राम

राम राम

व्यासेन भाषितमिदं

vyāsena bhāṣitamidaṁ

(फलश्रुति– phalaśruti)

रामाष्टकं पठति यः सुकरं सुपुण्यं

rām āṣṭakaṁ paṭh ati yaḥ su karaṁ su puṇyaṁ

व्यासेन भाषितमिदं श्रृणुते मनुष्यः ।

vyās ena bhāṣita midaṁ śṛṇu te manuṣ yaḥ ,

_______________ Today's Date

राम राम

राम राम

श्रृणुते मनुष्यः

śṛṇute manuṣyaḥ

(Benefits of Recitation)

Those who read this octet on Shrī Rāma—easy of comprehension, rife with virtues—which is composed by Sage Vyasa—

राम राम

राम
राम
राम
राम
राम
राम
राम
राम
राम
राम
राम
राम
राम
राम
राम
राम
राम
राम
राम
राम
राम
राम
राम
राम
राम
राम
राम
राम
राम
राम
राम
राम
राम
राम
राम
राम
राम
राम
राम
राम
राम
राम
राम
राम
राम
राम
राम
राम

विद्यां श्रियं

vidyāṁ śriyaṁ

_______________ Today's Date

राम राम

राम राम

विपुलसौख्यम

नन्तकीर्तिं

vipula saukhyama nantakīrtiṁ

राम राम

सम्प्राप्य देहविलये

samprāpya dehavilaye

राम राम

विद्यां श्रियं विपुलसौख्यमनन्तकीर्तिं

vidyāṁ śriyaṁ vipula saukhyam ananta kīrtiṁ

सम्प्राप्य देहविलये लभते च मोक्षम् ॥ ९ ॥

sam prāpya deha vilaye labh ate ca mokṣam .9.

________________ Today's Date

राम राम

राम राग राम राम राम राम राम राम राम राम राम राम राम

लभते च मोक्षम्

labhate ca mokṣam

—get abundant knowledge, plentiful wealth, ample happiness, oceanic fame; and they attain to the highest state in the end, gaining emancipation.

राम राम

इति श्रीव्यासविरचितं

iti śrīvyāsa viracitaṁ

राम राम

॥ इति श्रीव्यासविरचितं रामाष्टकं सम्पूर्णम् ॥

. iti śrī vyāsa viraci taṁ rām āṣṭakaṁ sam pūrṇam .

______ Today's Date

रामाष्टकं सम्पूर्णम्

rāmāṣṭakaṁ sampūrṇam

— Thus concludes śrī-rāmāṣṭakam composed by Shri Vyasa Maharishi —

राम राम

राम
राम
राम
राम
राम
राम
राम
राम
राम
राम
राम
राम
राम
राम
राम
राम
राम
राम
राम
राम
राम
राम
राम
राम
राम
राम
राम
राम
राम
राम
राम
राम
राम
राम
राम
राम
राम
राम
राम
राम
राम
राम
राम
राम
राम
राम
राम
राम

ॐ

श्रीरामाय

नमः

Today's Date

राम राम

राम राम

ॐ

श्रीरामभद्राय

नमः

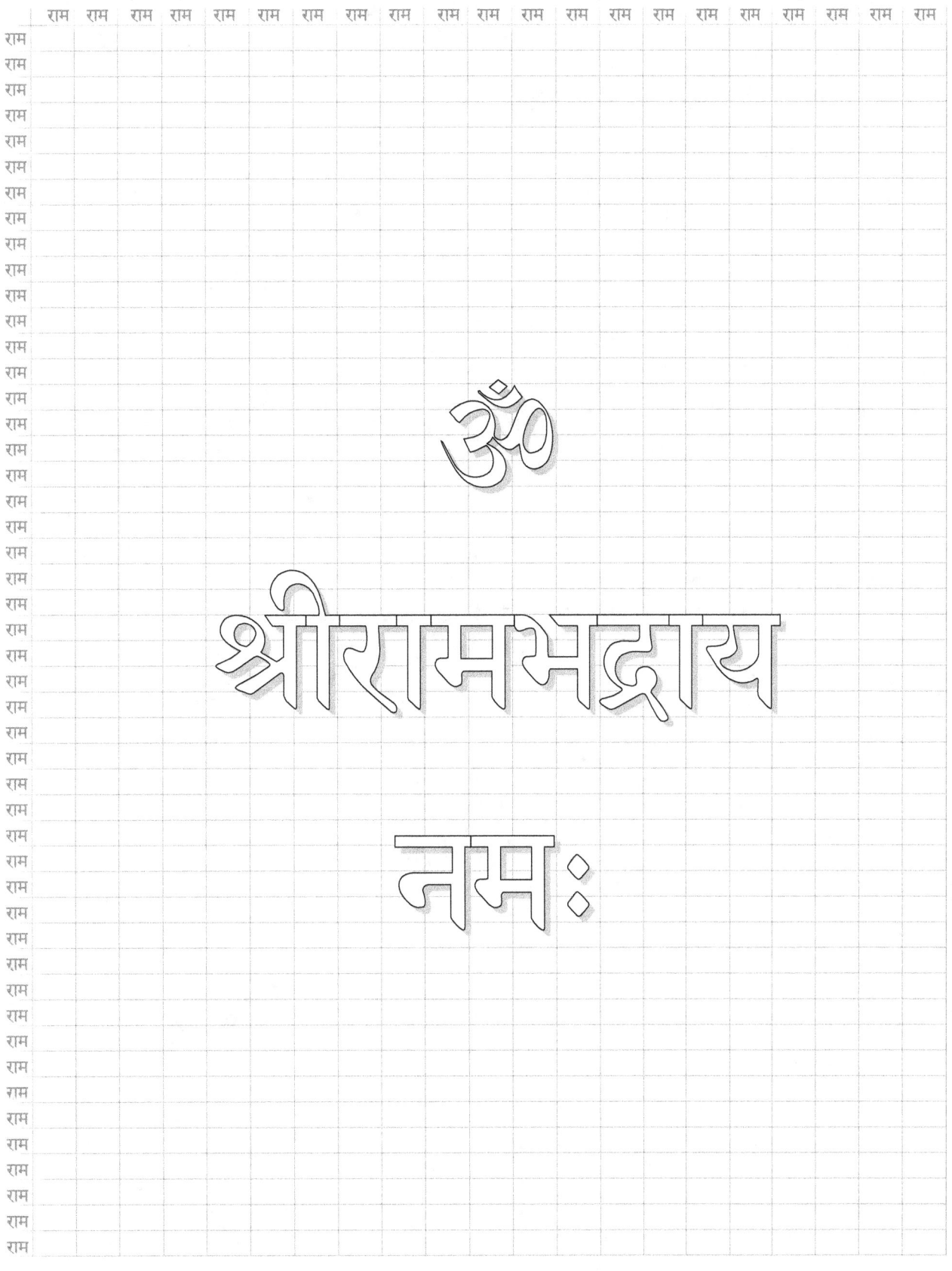

राम राम

राम
राम
राम
राम
राम
राम
राम
राम
राम
राम
राम
राम
राम
राम
राम
राम
राम
राम
राम
राम
राम
राम
राम
राम
राम
राम
राम
राम
राम
राम
राम
राम
राम
राम
राम
राम
राम
राम
राम
राम
राम
राम
राम
राम
राम
राम
राम
राम

ॐ

श्रीरामचंद्राय

नमः

__________________ Today's Date

राम राम

राम
राम
राम
राम
राम
राम
राम
राम
राम
राम
राम
राम
राम
राम
राम
राम
राम
राम
राम
राम
राम
राम
राम
राम
राम
राम
राम
राम
राम
राम
राम
राम
राम
राम
राम
राम
राम
राम
राम
राम
राम
राम
राम
राम
राम
राम
राम
राम

ॐ

जानकीवल्लभाय

नमः

राम राम

राम
राम
राम
राम
राम
राम
राम
राम
राम
राम
राम
राम
राम
राम
राम
राम
राम
राम
राम
राम
राम
राम
राम
राम
राम
राम
राम
राम
राम
राम
राम
राम
राम
राम
राम
राम
राम
राम
राम
राम
राम
राम
राम
राम
राम
राम
राम
राम

ॐ

सदाहनुमदाश्रिताय

नमः

__________ Today's Date

राम राम

राम
राम
राम
राम
राम
राम
राम
राम
राम
राम
राम
राम
राम
राम
राम
राम
राम
राम
राम
राम
राम
राम
राम
राम
राम
राम
राम
राम
राम
राम
राम
राम
राम
राम
राम
राम
राम
राम
राम
राम
राम
राम
राम
राम
राम
राम
राम
राम

ॐ

कौसल्येयाय

नमः

Today's Date : ____________________

राम राम

अथ

श्री

रामाष्टकम्

राम राम

________________ Today's Date

राम राम

राम
राम
राम
राम
राम
राम
राम
राम
राम
राम
राम
राम
राम
राम
राम
राम
राम
राम
राम
राम
राम
राम
राम
राम
राम
राम
राम
राम
राम
राम
राम
राम
राम
राम
राम
राम
राम
राम
राम
राम
राम
राम
राम
राम
राम
राम
राम
राम

atha śrī rāmāṣṭakam

(Now commences rāmāṣṭakam)

राम राम

राम राम

भजे विशेषसुन्दरं

bhaje viśeṣa sundaraṁ

Today's Date

राम राम

राम
राम
राम
राम
राम
राम
राम
राम
राम
राम
राम
राम
राम
राम
राम

समस्तपापखण्डनम्

राम
राम
राम
राम
राम
राम
राम
राम
राम
राम
राम
राम
राम
राम
राम
राम

samasta
pāpa
khaṇḍanam

राम
राम
राम
राम
राम
राम
राम
राम
राम
राम
राम
राम
राम
राम
राम
राम
राम

राम राम

राम राम

स्वभक्तचित्तरञ्जनं

svabhakta cittarañjanaṁ

भजे विशेषसुन्दरं समस्तपापखण्डनम् ।

bhaje viśeṣa sundaraṁ samasta pāpa khaṇḍa nam ,

स्वभक्तचित्तरञ्जनं सदैव राममद्वयम् ॥ १ ॥

sva bhakta citta rañja naṁ sa daiva rāmam ad vayam .1.

______________ Today's Date

राम राम

सदैव राममद्वयम्

sadaiva rāmam advayam

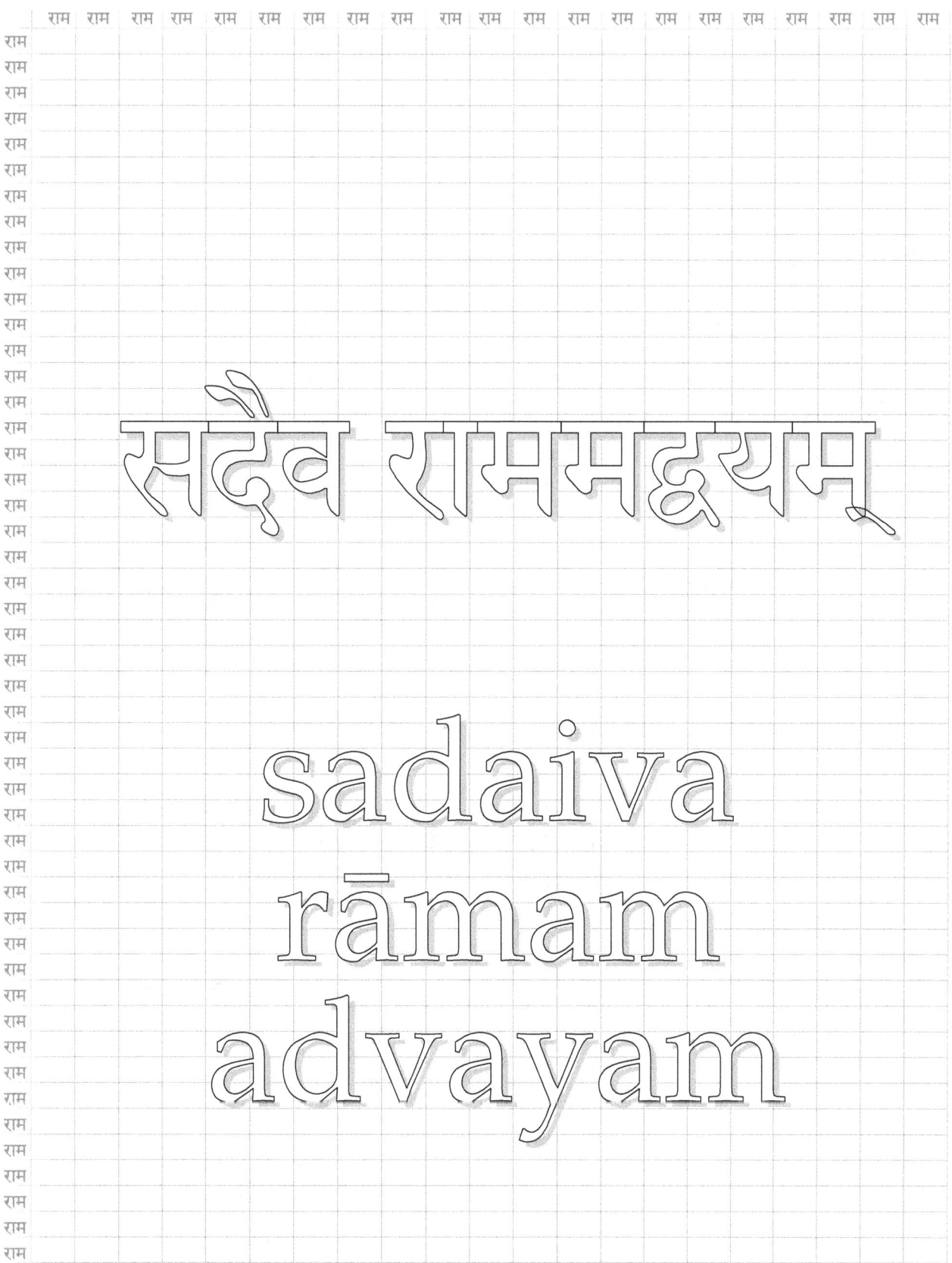

He, who annihilates all sins, who brings lasting joy to the hearts of His devotees, O mind, dwell upon Him—the supremely beautiful Lord: Shrī Rāma, the One-God second to none.

Today's Date : ____________________

राम राम

राम राम

जटाकलापशोभितं

jaṭākalāpa śobhitaṁ

Today's Date

राम राम

राम
राम
राम
राम
राम
राम
राम
राम
राम
राम
राम
राम
राम
राम

समस्तपापनाशकम्

राम
राम
राम
राम
राम
राम
राम
राम
राम
राम

samasta
pāpa
nāśakam

राम
राम
राम
राम
राम
राम

राम राम

राम राम

स्वभक्तभीतिभङ्गनं

svabhakta
bhīti
bhaṅjanaṁ

जटाकलापशोभितं समस्तपापनाशकम् ।
jaṭā kalā paśo bhitaṁ samasta pāpa nāśa kam ,
स्वभक्तभीतिभङ्गनं भजे ह राममद्वयम् ॥ २ ॥
sva bhakta bhīti bhaṅja naṁ bhaje ha rāmam ad vayam .2.

Today's Date

भजे ह राममद्वयम्

bhaje ha rāmam advayam

He, who is the destroyers of sins, who dispels all fears from the hearts of His devotees, O mind, dwell upon His resplendent form with matted hair—Him Shrī Rāma, the One-God second to none.

Today's Date : ____________________

राम राम

राम राम

निजस्वरूपबोधकं

nija svarūpa bodhakaṁ

Today's Date

राम राम

कृपाकरं भवापहम्

kṛpākaraṁ bhavāpaham

राम राम

राम राम

राम राम

समं शिवं निरञ्जनं

samaṁ śivaṁ nirañjanaṁ

निजस्वरूपबोधकं कृपाकरं भवापहम् ।

nija svarūpa bodha kaṁ kṛpā karaṁ bhav āpaham ,

समं शिवं निरञ्जनं भजे ह राममद्वयम् ॥ ३ ॥

samaṁ śivaṁ nirañja naṁ bhaje ha rāmam ad vayam .3.

________________ Today's Date

राम राम

राम राम

भजे ह राममद्वयम्

bhaje ha rāmam advayam

Through whom we become enlightened of our true nature, who is most merciful & kind, who takes us across this intimidating ocean-like world, who is equitable to all, who is ever auspicious, ever pure—O mind, dwell upon the ocean of tranquility Shrī Rāma, the One-God second to none.

Today's Date : ______________

राम राम

राम राम

सहप्रपञ्चकल्पितं

sahaprapañca kalpitaṁ

Today's Date

राम राम

राम राग राम राम राम राम राम राम राम राम राम राम राम राम राम राम

ह्यनामरूपवास्तवम्

hyanāmarūpa vāstavam

राम राम

राम राम

निराकृतिं निरामयं

nirākṛtiṁ nirāmayaṁ

सहप्रपञ्चकल्पितं ह्यनामरूपवास्तवम् ।
saha pra pañca kalpitaṁ hya nāma rūpa vāsta vam ,
निराकृतिं निरामयं भजे ह राममद्वयम् ॥ ४ ॥
nir ākṛtiṁ nir āmayaṁ bhaje ha rāmam ad vayam .4.

____________ Today's Date

राम राम

राम राम

भजे ह राममद्वयम्

bhaje ha rāmam advayam

Of His will who took this illusory form—who is the world, from whom is the world, who has the world within Him—who is the Absolute-Truth, without a name, without a form, free from blemishes, shortcomings, faults—I worship Him: Shri Rāma, the One-God second to none.

राम राम

राम
राम
राम
राम
राम
राम
राम
राम
राम
राम
राम
राम
राम
राम
राम
राम
राम
राम
राम
राम
राम
राम
राम
राम
राम
राम
राम
राम
राम
राम
राम
राम
राम
राम
राम
राम
राम
राम
राम
राम
राम
राम
राम
राम
राम
राम
राम
राम

निष्प्रपञ्चनिर्विकल्प

nisprapañca nirvikalpa

______________ Today's Date

राम राम

राम
राम
राम
राम
राम
राम
राम
राम
राम
राम
राम
राम
राम
राम
राम
राम
राम

निर्मलं निरामयम्

राम
राम
राम
राम
राम
राम
राम
राम
राम
राम
राम
राम
राम
राम
राम
राम
राम
राम
राम

nirmalaṁ

राग
राम
राम
राम
राम

nirāmayam

राग
राम
राम
राम
राम
राम
राम

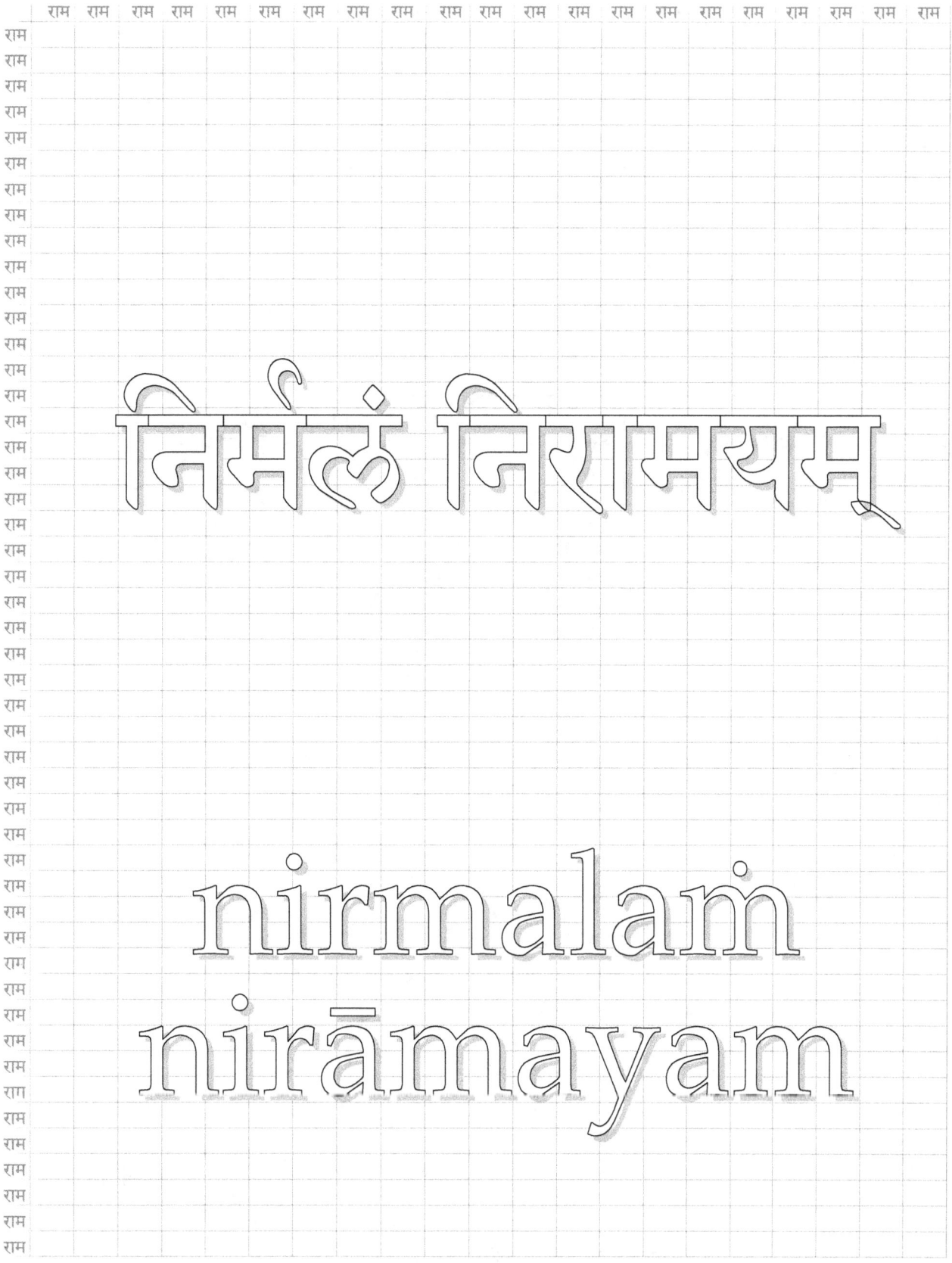

राम राम

राम राम

चिदेकरूपसन्ततं

cidekarūpa santataṁ

निष्प्रपञ्चनिर्विकल्पनिर्मलं निरामयम् ॥

niṣ prapañca nir vikalpa nir malaṁ nirāma yam.

चिदेकरूपसन्ततं भजे ह राममद्वयम् ॥ ५ ॥

cid eka rūpa santa taṁ bhaje ha rāmam ad vayam .5.

Today's Date

राम राम

राम राम

भजे ह राममद्वयम्

bhaje ha rāmam advayam

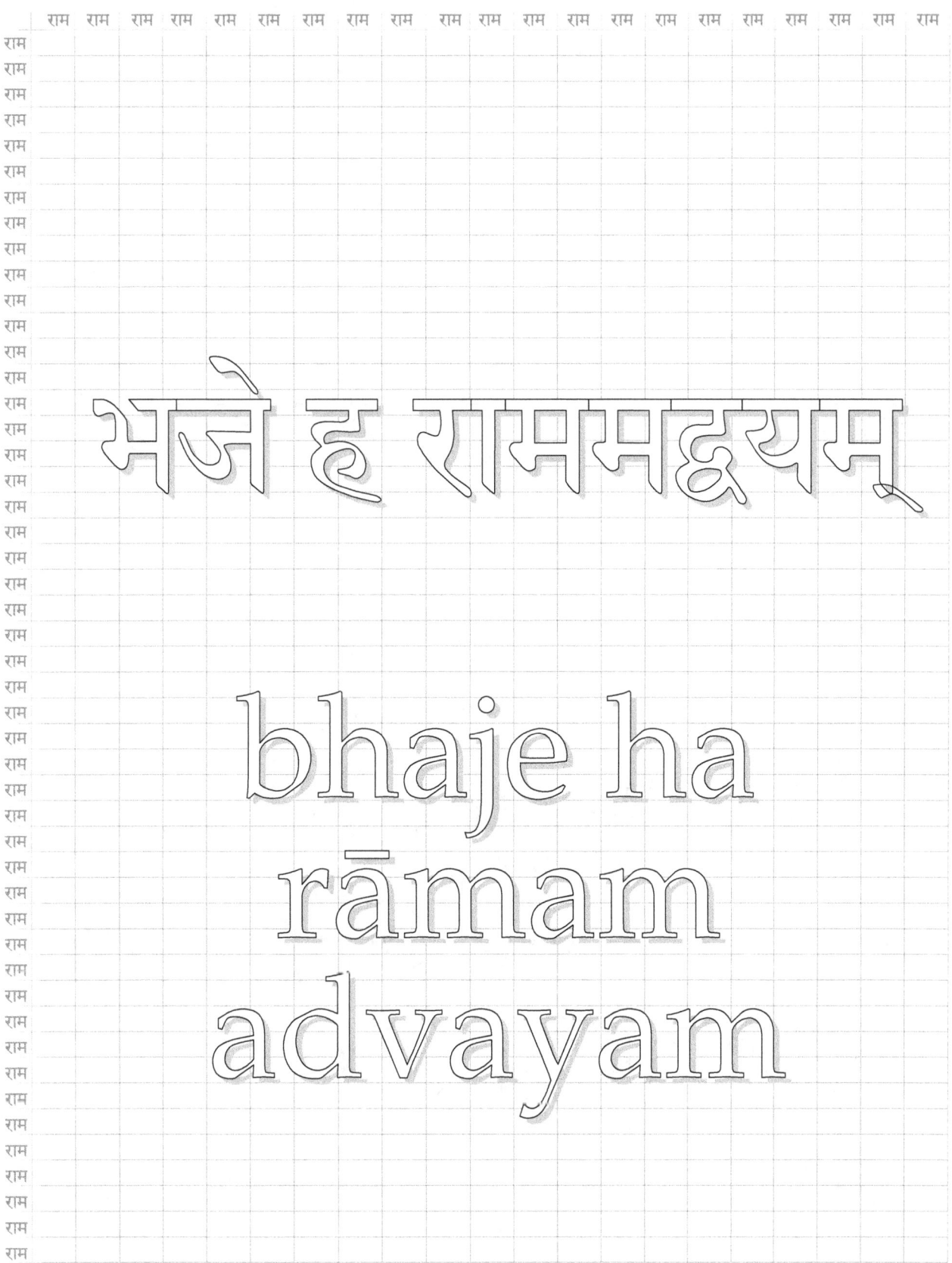

O mind, dwell on Rāma—the imperishable essence beyond creation, beyond the worldly dualities, untainted, the ever pure, unsullied of worldly maladies, the absolute Truth that stands as the all-abiding essence within everything—O mind, worship Rāma, the One-God second to none.

राम राम

राम
राम
राम
राम
राम
राम
राम
राम
राम
राम
राम
राम
राम
राम
राम
राम
राम
राम
राम
राम
राम
राम
राम
राम
राम
राम
राम
राम
राम
राम
राम
राम
राम
राम
राम
राम
राम
राम
राम
राम
राम
राम
राम
राम
राम
राम
राम
राम

भवाब्धिपोतरूपकं

bhavābdhi
pota
rūpakaṁ

_______________ Today's Date

ह्यशेषदेहकल्पितम्

hyaśeṣadeha
kalpitam

राम राम

राम
राम
राम
राम
राम
राम
राम
राम
राम
राम
राम
राम
राम
राम
राम
राम
राम
राम
राम
राम
राम
राम
राम
राम
राम
राम
राम
राम
राम
राम
राम
राम
राम
राम
राम
राम
राम
राम
राम
राम
राम
राम
राम
राम
राम
राम
राम
राम

गुणाकरं कृपाकरं

guṇākaraṁ kṛpākaraṁ

भवाब्धिपोतरूपकं ह्यशेषदेहकल्पितम् ।

bhav ābdhi pota rūpa kaṁ hya śeṣa deha kal pitam ,

गुणाकरं कृपाकरं भजे ह राममद्वयम् ॥ ६ ॥

guṇā karaṁ kṛpā karaṁ bhaje ha rāmam ad vayam .6.

______________ Today's Date

राम राम

राम
राम
राम
राम
राम
राम
राम
राम
राम
राम
राम
राम
राम
राम
राम
राम
राम
राम
राम
राम
राम
राम
राम
राम
राम
राम
राम
राम
राम
राम
राम
राम
राम
राम
राम
राम
राम
राम
राम
राग
राम
राम
राम
राम
राम
राम
राम
राम

भजे ह राममद्वयम्

bhaje ha rāmam advayam

Who is the bark to cross the ocean of worldly existence, the One-shining Truth behind all beingness, doer behind all activity—Him venerate: the all-merciful all-gracious fount of virtues Shrī Rāma, the One-God second to none.

राम राम

राम राम

महावाक्यबोधकै

mahāvākya
bodhakair

विराजमनवाक्पदैः

virājamana vākpadaiḥ

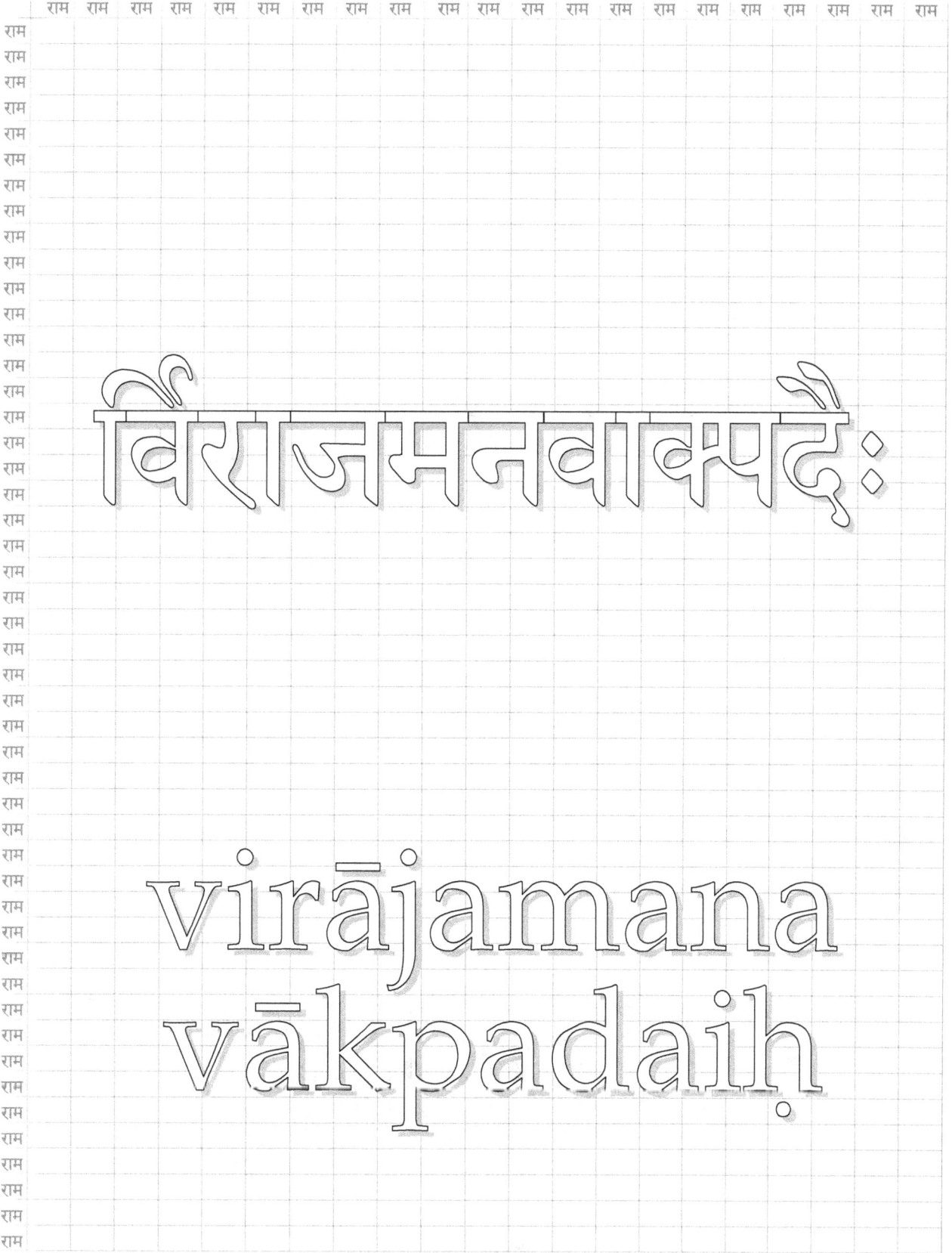

राम राम

राम राम

परब्रह्म व्यापकं

parabrahma vyāpakaṁ

महावाक्यबोधकैर्विराजमनवाक्पदैः ।
mahā vākya bodha kair virāja mana vāk padaiḥ ,
परब्रह्म व्यापकं भजे ह राममद्वयम् ॥ ७ ॥
para brahma vyāpa kaṁ bhaje ha rāmam ad vayam .7.

_______________ Today's Date

राम राम

राम राम

भजे ह राममद्वयम्

bhaje ha rāmam advayam

Worship Shrī Rāma—the essence of Vedanta, whose glory irradiates through the great Vedic Sayings, who is the Supreme all-pervading Brahmm diffused throughout the universe—the Exalted One Rāma, the One-God second to none.

राम राम

राम राम

शिवप्रदं सुखप्रदं

śivapradaṁ sukhapradaṁ

______________ Today's Date

भवच्छिदं भ्रमापहम्

bhavacchidaṁ
bhramāpaham

राम राम

राम राम

विराजमानदैशिकं

virājamāna daiśikaṁ

शिवप्रदं सुखप्रदं भवच्छिदं भ्रमापहम् ।
śiva pradaṁ sukha pradaṁ bhav acchid aṁ bhram āpaham ,
विराजमानदैशिकं भजे ह राममद्वयम् ॥ ८ ॥
virāja māna daiśik aṁ bhaje ha rāmam ad vayam .8.

_______________ Today's Date

भजे ह राममद्वयम्

bhaje ha rāmam advayam

Who confers felicity and prosperity, who rents asunder all worldly bondages, who is beyond the delusive Māyā, who is the Supreme-Self dwelling within His own resplendency—Him worship, Shrī Rāma, the One-God second to none.

Today's Date : ____________________

राम राम

रामाष्टकं पठति यः

rāmāṣṭakaṁ paṭhati yaḥ

राम राम

_______________ Today's Date

राम राम

राम
राम
राम
राम
राम
राम
राम
राम
राम
राम
राम
राम
राम
राम

सुकरं सुपुण्यं

राम
राम
राम
राम
राम
राम
राम
राम
राम
राम
राम
राम
राम
राम
राम
राम
राम
राम

sukaraṁ

राम
राम
राम
राम
राग
राम

supuṇyaṁ

राम
राम
राम
राम
राम
राम
राम
राम
राम
राम

राम राम

राम राम

व्यासेन भाषितामिदं

vyāsena bhāṣitamidaṁ

(फलश्रुति – phalaśruti)

रामाष्टकं पठति यः सुकरं सुपुण्यं

rām āṣṭakaṁ paṭh ati yaḥ su karaṁ su puṇyaṁ

व्यासेन भाषितमिदं श्रृणुते मनुष्यः ।

vyās ena bhāṣita midaṁ śṛṇu te manuṣ yaḥ ,

_____________ Today's Date

राम राम

श्रृणुते मनुष्यः

śṛṇute manuṣyaḥ

(Benefits of Recitation)

Those who read this octet on Shrī Rāma—easy of comprehension, rife with virtues—which is composed by Sage Vyasa—

राम राम

राम
राम
राम
राम
राम
राम
राम
राम
राम
राम
राम
राम
राम
राम
राम
राम
राम
राम
राम
राम
राम
राम
राम
राम
राम
राम
राम
राम
राम
राम
राम
राम
राम
राम
राम
राम
राम
राम
राम
राम
राम
राम
राम
राम
राम
राम
राम
राम

विद्यां श्रियं

vidyāṁ
śriyaṁ

______________ Today's Date

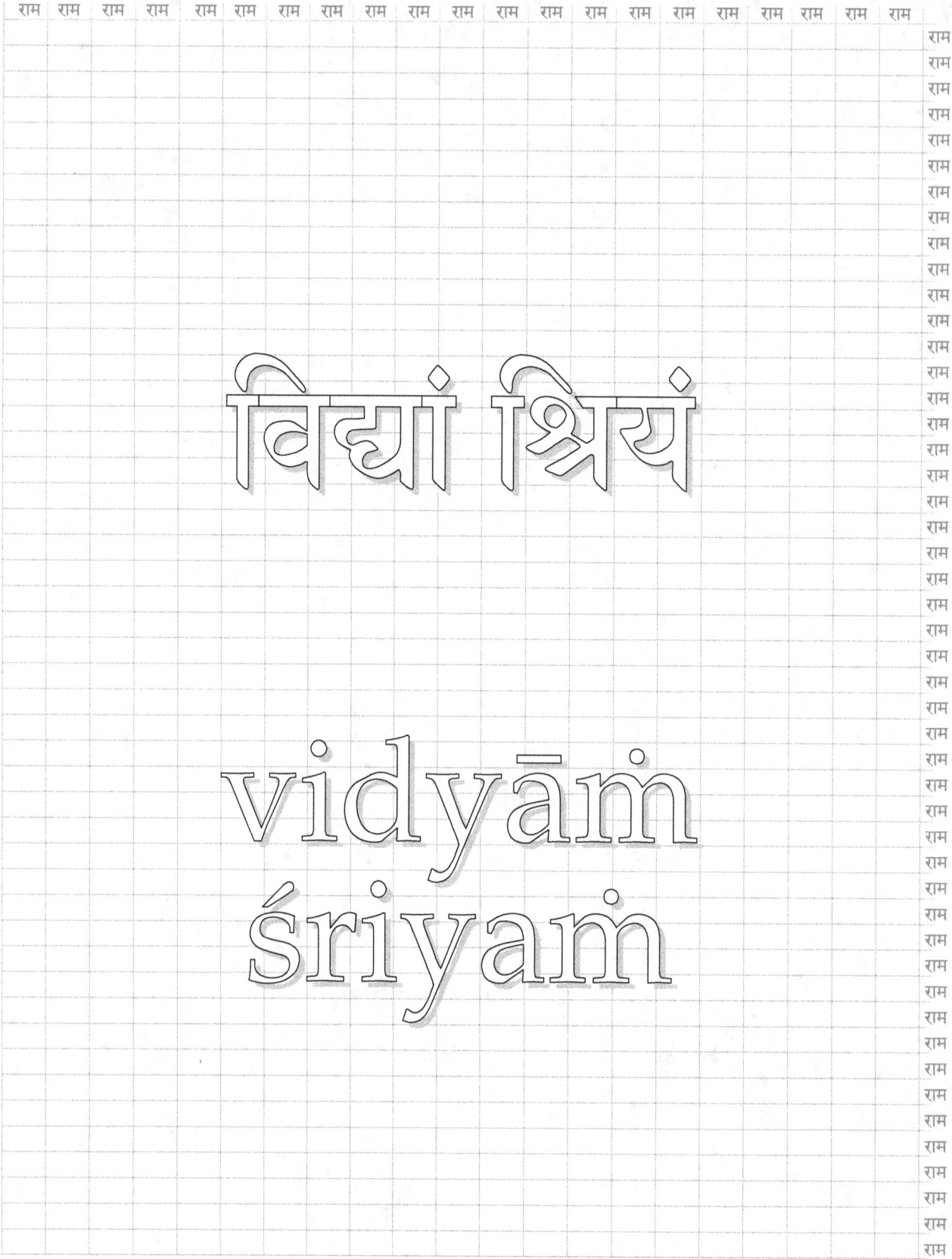

विपुलसौख्यम

नन्तकीर्तिं

vipula
saukhyama
nantakīrtiṁ

राम राम

राम राम

सम्प्राप्य देहविलये

samprāpya dehavilaye

विद्यां श्रियं विपुलसौख्यमनन्तकीर्तिं

vidyāṁ śriyaṁ vipula saukhyam ananta kīrtiṁ

सम्प्राप्य देहविलये लभते च मोक्षम् ॥ ९ ॥

sam prāpya deha vilaye labh ate ca mokṣam .9.

_______________ Today's Date

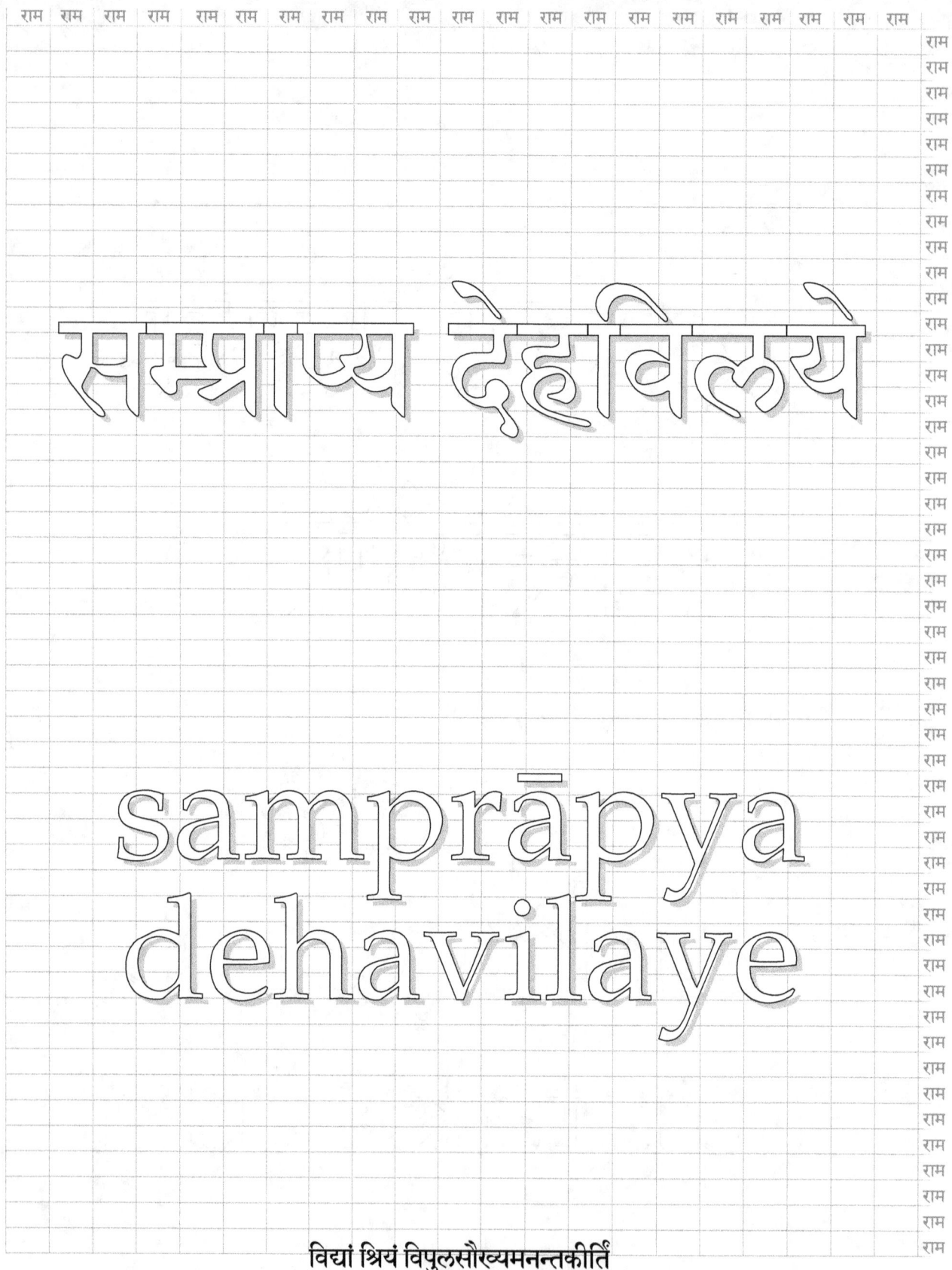

राम राम

राम राम

लभते च मोक्षम्

labhate ca mokṣam

—get abundant knowledge, plentiful wealth, ample happiness, oceanic fame; and they attain to the highest state in the end, gaining emancipation.

राम राम

इति श्रीव्यासविरचितं

iti śrīvyāsa viracitaṁ

राम राम

॥ इति श्रीव्यासविरचितं रामाष्टकं सम्पूर्णम् ॥

. iti śrī vyāsa viraci taṁ rām āṣṭakaṁ sam pūrṇam .

_____________ Today's Date

रामाष्टकं सम्पूर्णम्

rāmāṣṭakaṁ sampūrṇam

— Thus concludes śrī-rāmāṣṭakam composed by Shri Vyasa Maharishi —

राम राम

रामभद्र

राम
राम
राम
राम
राम
राम
राम
राम
राम
राम
राम
राम
राम
राम
राम
राम
राम
राम
राम
राम
राम
राम
राम
राम
राम
राम
राम
राम
राम
राम
राम
राम
राम
राम
राम
राम
राम
राम
राम
राम
राम
राम
राम
राम
राम
राम
राम
राम

________________Today's Date

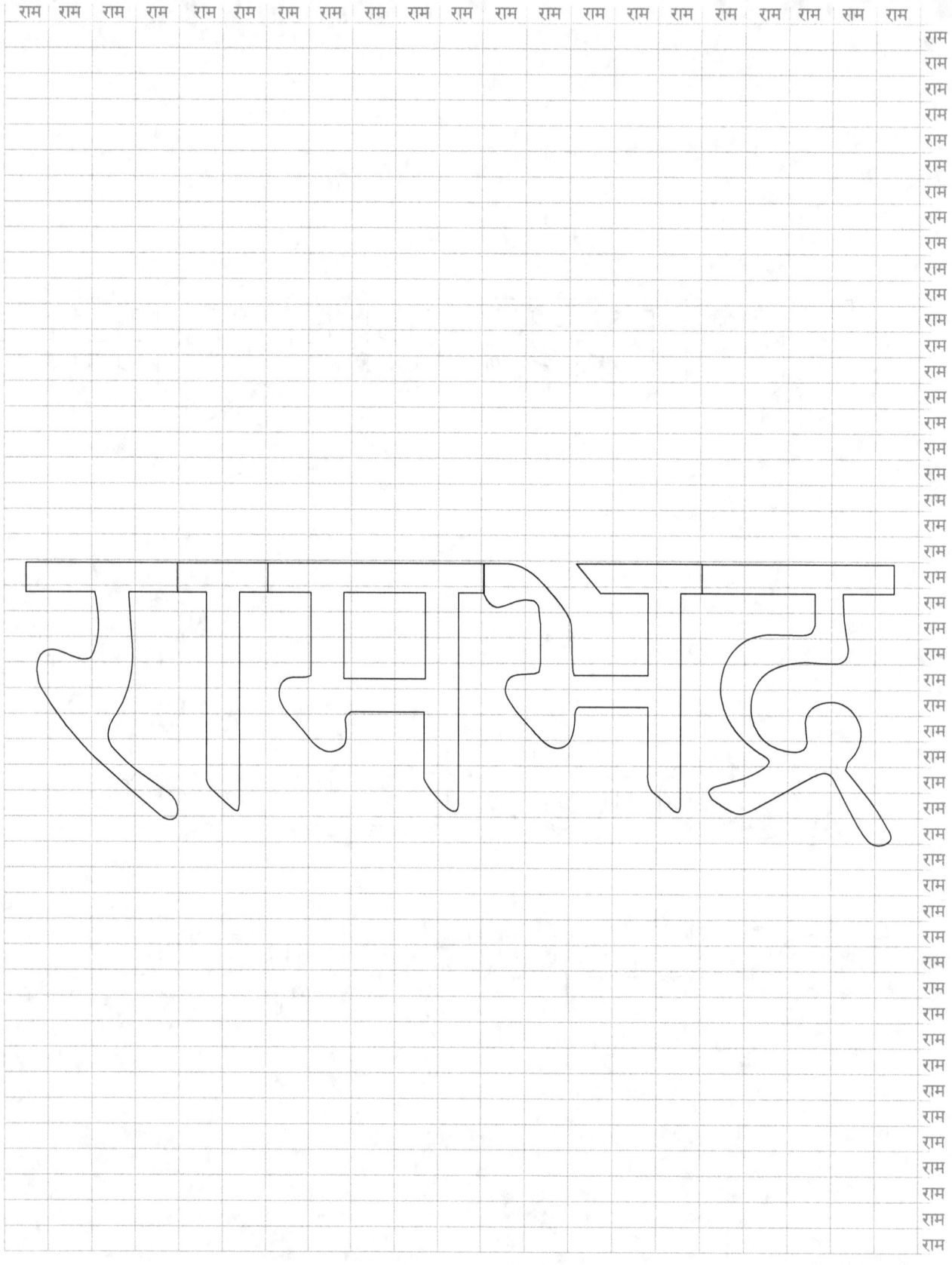

राम राम

राम
राम
राम
राम
राम
राम
राम
राम
राम
राम
राम
राम
राम
राम
राम
राम
राम
राम
राम
राम
राम
राम
राम
राम
राम
राम
राम
राम
राम
राम
राम
राम
राम
राम
राम
राम
राम
राम
राम
राम
राम
राग
राम
राम
राम
राम
राम
राम

रामचंद्र

Today's Date : ____________________

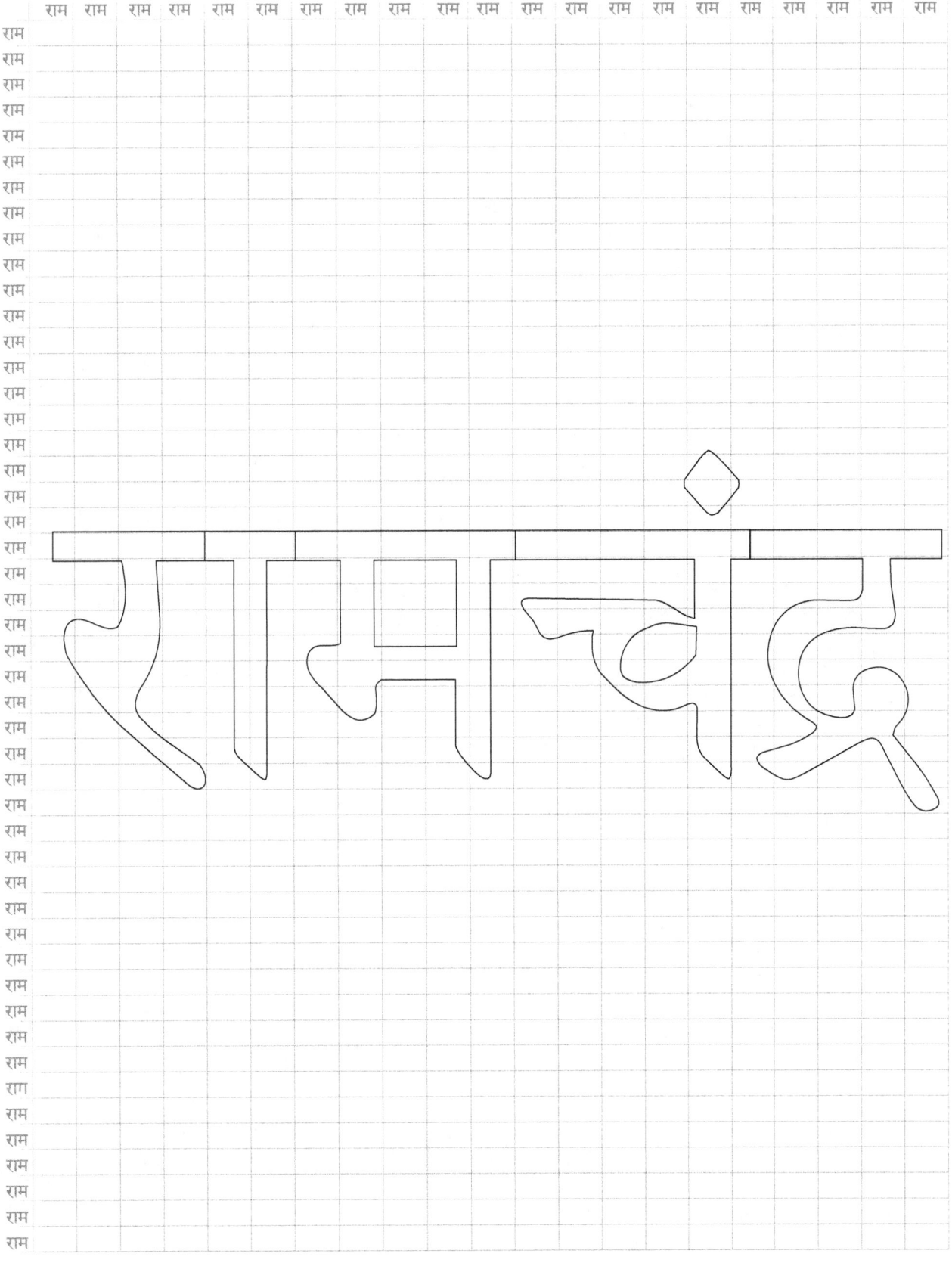

राम राम

ॐ राम

राम
राम
राम
राम
राम
राम
राम
राम
राम
राम
राम
राम
राम
राम
राम
राम
राम
राम
राम
राम
राम
राम
राम
राम
राम
राम
राम
राम
राम
राम
राम
राम
राम
राम
राम
राम
राम
राम
राम
राम
राम
राम
राम
राम
राम
राम
राम
राम

_______________ Today's Date

राम राम

राम
राम
राम
राम
राम
राम
राम
राम
राम
राम
राम
राम
राम
राम
राम
राम
राम
राम
राम
राम
राम
राम
राम
राम
राम
राम
राम
राम
राम
राम
राम
राम
राम
राम
राम
राम
राम
राम
राम
राम
राम
राम
राम
राम
राम
राम
राम
राम

रां राम

राम राम

राम
राम
राम
राम
राम
राम
राम
राम
राम
राम
राम
राम
राम
राम
राम
राम
राम
राम
राम
राम
राम
राम
राम
राम
राम
राम
राम
राम
राम
राम
राम
राम
राम
राम
राम
राम
राम
राम
राम
राम
राम
राम
राम
राम
राम
राम
राम
राम

________________ Today's Date

राम राम

राम
राम
राम
राम
राम
राम
राम
राम
राम
राम
राम
राम
राम
राम
राम
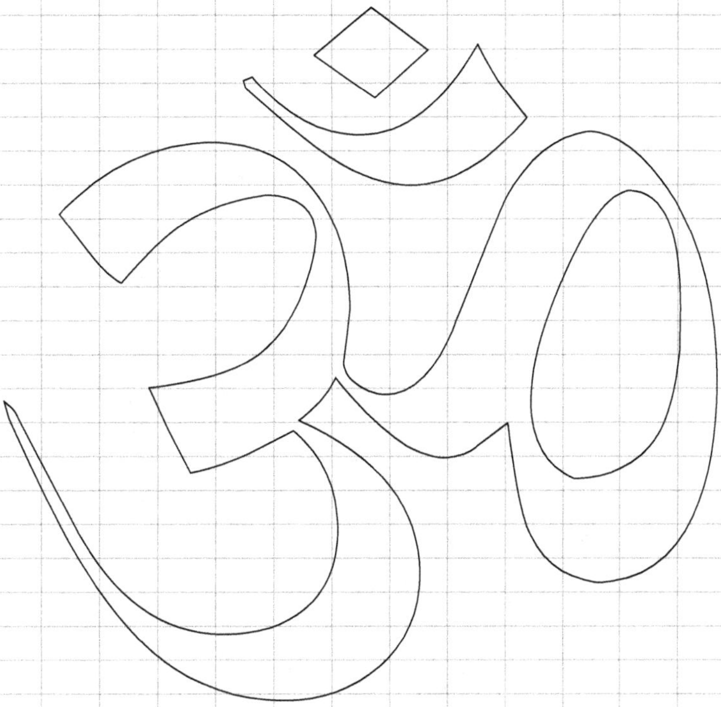
राम
राम
राम
राम
राम
राम
राम
राम
राम
राम
राम
राम
राम
राम
राम
राम
राम
राम
राम
राम
राम
राम
राम
राम
राम
राम
राग
राम
राम
राम
राम
राम
राम

Today's Date : ____________________

राम राम

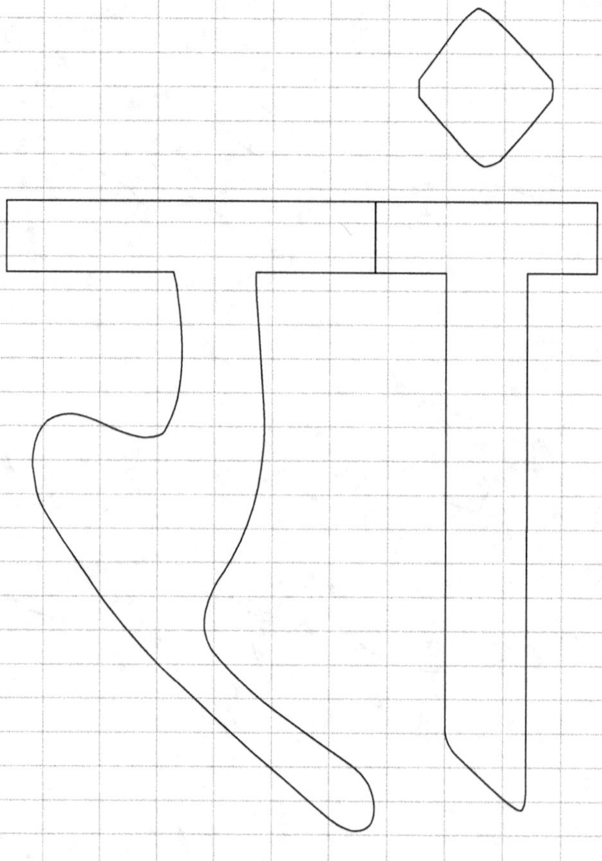

राम
राम
राम
राम
राम
राम
राम
राम
राम
राम
राम
राम
राम
राम
राम
राम
राम
राम
राम
राम
राम
राम
राम
राम
राम
राम
राम
राम
राम
राम
राम
राम
राम
राम
राम
राम
राम
राम
राम
राम
राम
राम
राम
राम
राम
राम
राम
राम

__________ Today's Date

श्रीरामाष्टकम्
śrī-rāmāṣṭakam

सीताराम सीताराम सीताराम सीताराम सीताराम

भजे विशेषसुन्दरं समस्तपापखण्डनम् ।

bhaje viśeṣa-sundaraṁ samasta-pāpa-khaṇḍa-nam ,

स्वभक्तचित्तरञ्जनं सदैव राममद्वयम् ॥ १ ॥

sva-bhakta-citta-rañja-naṁ sa-daiva rāmam-ad-vayam .1.

He, who annihilates all sins, who brings lasting joy to the hearts of His devotees, O mind, dwell upon Him—the supremely beautiful Lord: Shrī Rāma, the One-God second to none.

जटाकलापशोभितं समस्तपापनाशकम् ।

jaṭā-kalā-paśo-bhitaṁ samasta-pāpa-nāśa-kam ,

स्वभक्तभीतिभञ्जनं भजे ह राममद्वयम् ॥ २ ॥

sva-bhakta-bhīti-bhañja-naṁ bhaje ha rāmam-ad-vayam .2.

He, who is the destroyers of sins, who dispels all fears from the hearts of His devotees, O mind, dwell upon His resplendent form with matted hair—Him Shrī Rāma, the One-God second to none.

निजस्वरूपबोधकं कृपाकरं भवापहम् ।

nija-svarūpa-bodha-kaṁ kṛpā-karaṁ bhav-āpaham ,

समं शिवं निरञ्जनं भजे ह राममद्वयम् ॥ ३ ॥

samaṁ śivaṁ nirañja-naṁ bhaje ha rāmam-ad-vayam .3.

Through whom we become enlightened of our true nature, who is most merciful & kind, who takes us across this intimidating ocean-like world, who is equitable to all, who is ever auspicious, ever pure—O mind, dwell upon the ocean of tranquility Shrī Rāma, the One-God second to none.

सहप्रपञ्चकल्पितं ह्यनामरूपवास्तवम् ।

saha-pra-pañca-kalpitaṁ hya-nāma-rūpa-vāsta-vam ,

निराकृतिं निरामयं भजे ह राममद्वयम् ॥ ४ ॥

nir-ākṛtiṁ nir-āmayaṁ bhaje ha rāmam-ad-vayam .4.

Of his will who took this illusory form—who is the world, from whom is the world, who has the world within Him—who is the Absolute-Truth, without a name, without a form, free from blemishes, shortcomings, faults—I worship Him: Shri Rāma, the One-God second to none.

निष्प्रपञ्चनिर्विकल्पनिर्मलं निरामयम् ॥

niṣ-prapañca-nir-vikalpa-nir-malaṁ nirāma-yam.

चिदेकरूपसन्ततं भजे ह राममद्वयम् ॥ ५ ॥

cid-eka-rūpa-santa-taṁ bhaje ha rāmam-ad-vayam .5.

O mind, dwell on Rāma—the imperishable essence beyond creation, beyond the worldly dualities, untainted, the ever pure, unsullied of worldly maladies, the absolute Truth that stands as the all-abiding essence within everything—O mind, worship Rāma, the One-God second to none.

भवाब्धिपोतरूपकं ह्यशेषदेहकल्पितम् ।
bhav-ābdhi-pota-rūpa-kaṁ hya-śeṣa-deha-kal-pitam ,
गुणाकरं कृपाकरं भजे ह राममद्वयम् ॥ ६ ॥
guṇā-karaṁ kṛpā-karaṁ bhaje ha rāmam-ad-vayam .6.

Who is the bark to cross the ocean of worldly existence, the One-shining Truth behind all beingness, doer behind all activity—Him venerate: the all-merciful all-gracious fount of virtues Shrī Rāma, the One-God second to none.

महावाक्यबोधकैर्विराजमनवाक्पदैः ।
mahā-vākya-bodha-kair-virāja-mana-vāk-padaiḥ ,
परब्रह्म व्यापकं भजे ह राममद्वयम् ॥ ७ ॥
para-brahma vyāpa-kaṁ bhaje ha rāmam-ad-vayam .7.

Worship Shrī Rāma—the essence of Vedanta, whose glory irradiates through the great Vedic Sayings, who is the Supreme all-pervading Brahmm diffused throughout the universe—the Exalted One Rāma, the One-God second to none.

शिवप्रदं सुखप्रदं भवच्छिदं भ्रमापहम् ।
śiva-pradaṁ sukha-pradaṁ bhav-acchid-aṁ bhram-āpaham ,
विराजमानदैशिकं भजे ह राममद्वयम् ॥ ८ ॥
virāja-māna-daiśik-aṁ bhaje ha rāmam-ad-vayam .8.

Who confers felicity and prosperity, who rents asunder all worldly bondages, who is beyond the delusive Māyā, who is the Supreme-Self dwelling within His own resplendency—Him I worship, Shrī Rāma, the One-God second to none.

रामाष्टकं पठति यः सुकरं सुपुण्यं
rām-āṣṭakaṁ paṭh-ati yaḥ su-karaṁ su-puṇyaṁ
व्यासेन भाषितमिदं शृणुते मनुष्यः ।
vyās-ena bhāṣita-midaṁ śṛṇu-te manuṣ-yaḥ ,
विद्यां श्रियं विपुलसौख्यमनन्तकीर्तिं
vidyāṁ śriyaṁ vipula-saukhyam-ananta-kīrtiṁ
सम्प्राप्य देहविलये लभते च मोक्षम् ॥ ९ ॥
sam-prāpya deha-vilaye labh-ate ca mokṣam .9.

Those who read this octet on Shrī Rāma—easy of comprehension, rife with virtues—which is composed by Sage Vyasa—get abundant knowledge, plentiful wealth, ample happiness, oceanic fame; and they attain to the highest state in the end, gaining emancipation.

॥ इति श्रीव्यासविरचितं रामाष्टकं सम्पूर्णम् ॥

. iti śrī-vyāsa-viraci-taṁ rām-āṣṭakaṁ sam-pūrṇam .

— Thus ends the Ramashtakam composed by Shri Vyasa Maharishi —

[Author of this Original Sanskrit Hymn is: Shrī Vyāsa-Deva (Pre-historic Sage). Translator: Sushma]

www.ingramcontent.com/pod-product-compliance
Lightning Source LLC
Chambersburg PA
CBHW080026130526
44591CB00037B/2683